Conquering The Gifted Curse of Bipolarism

Volume 1:
Gray Poopon

By David Zosel

Dedication

I dedicate "Gray Poopon" to John Rehkamp and all of the lost ones who suffer from mental illnesses, who are misunderstood and misguided. John Rehkamp was a successful gregarious man, who was a great husband, and father that lit up every room that he walked into. May his spirit live on.

For Hagar.

You gave me the final push of courage that I needed to publish this book series when you gave me the feeling of balance in my life. You pushed me off the ledge of my lunatic fringe, giving me the power to fly. Until we meet again, may G-d hold you in the palm of his hand.

Must Read Prologue:

This is my confession of acceptance to the world. I suffer from the severe Bipolar disorder that I have and it has really held me back thus far in my mid-twenties. Do not feel sorry for me because this is my "Gifted Curse".

After finally growing tired of waking up everyday feeling like a different person during my non-medicated stint of bipolar disorder, I made a change for myself because it was the right time in my life to move forward to nullify the constant imbalance in my life.

Four years ago I started to notice a higher power that was comparable to when a superhero discovers his power. My friends and family viewed it differently as I fell into serious insomnia, racing thoughts, decreased appetite, and my mouth could never keep up with how fast my brain was moving.

At that time, I thought that this was the greatest thing ever, seriously. Despite my physical state, my life was a holiday. I could access every part of my brain, and at that time in my life I thought that I could finally put it all together and use it to conquer the world.

The way I viewed my changes was as if I had become a super mutant in X-Men. My friends and family became very concerned about me. I wasn't capable of knowing the reality that I was in because of my delusional mania.

Suddenly, I was rapidly increasing from doing five projects to doing 20 of them simultaneously. There was one point that I kept dropping things in my apartment going from one task to another. I was walking back and forth fleeing from one thing to another, finding myself always out of breath. From working, financing a short film, promoting a Kickstarter, moving, starting a business, writing a screenplay, and with the list that ensured I was ready to take over the world.

When inspiration struck every five seconds, I furiously wrote them down in a booklet. Now, I can't even read the maniacal handwriting that is in that book. Then, I started breaking glasses, furniture, and getting paper cuts accidentally.

It became clear to everyone, except me.

They told me to get help, and I refused to listen. I was flourishing and no one could stop me from reaching my potential.

It is hard to recollect the phone calls or what my diabolical plan was to take over the world through filmmaking, entrepreneurship, owning a 747 private jet filled with champagne and perfect 10 models, and all the excess that I could achieve at age 21.

Darkness struck and I do not remember any of the details of the 48 hours that transitioned into a very spine-chilling life chapter.

Then I woke up in a detained room in a hospital. For the next part of my life, I spent time in a psychiatric ward at North Memorial Hospital being informed that I had type I Bipolar Disorder.

I couldn't accept it.

Every day I tried to get out of that wretched place trying to convince everyone that I was fine. Compared to everyone else, I was happy and they were all sad. But, you cannot compare your situation to others, never.

After being pumped with many drugs, I vowed to never go back again. The aftermath of being released to the outside showed me that life wouldn't be the same as I found myself being reborn into something that I didn't understand.

I scared all of my close friends away. The only people that I had in my circle were my therapist and family. I am thankful that I had my family because people who go through this sometimes don't even have that.

After months of medication, hair loss, weight gain, and medically induced suicidal thoughts, slowly I eased myself back into a gray life. Then I decided to stop medicating in order to discover who I truly was.

Since then I have documented all of my tendencies with the help of my therapist. Last year in the fall of 2016, I learned that bad things happen in threes. With all of the natural things that I did to combat Bipolar Disorder, I could not handle insomnia, delusions, paranoia, stress, and all of the brewing mania. With one slip up, I could go back to the hospital. With me seeing these changes, knowing myself better than everyone else, I made the decision to commit to a medication that I had never tried before, Lamictal.

I call it "Gray Poopon", the title of my first volume in my book series, "Conquering the Gifted Curse of Bipolarism". This is the world first written in real time memoir, as I documented every change that I went through with medication along with my life and how I handled my problems. The etymology for the title came from the fear of what medication can do. I didn't want to lose my productivity, bravado, and ambition. I am horrified of feeling gray and pooped on by Lamictal. All I wanted in my life was to feel like a fresh jar of Grey Poupon.

Reality is now the hard part that is beginning. Now I am sharing with people my three-part documented journey with medication, self-betterment, and life problem solving to find balance in the life of a swaying monstrous mindset. I have never been so scared, but I am giving it all to the world.

I am sharing my journey to provide vital information, swallowing my pride and shallow secrets. I need to do this in order to help people with mental illnesses. Releasing my problems to the world is going to help students, psychiatrists, and people understand their loved ones with mental health issues. I just want to help someone because I didn't have any guide to this and maybe this will be the perfect help to someone. After reading numerous books, memoirs, stories, and blogs, I really wished that I had something as specific as this because taking prescription medication is a terrifying thing.

This is my "Gifted Curse" and I have accepted who I am. Despite the adversity of it seriously holding me back, I have great advantages and it is no excuse.

"I am now learning to get my life on, harnessing this X-men power by the hour, getting my superhero on, with Charles Xavier naming me The Gray Poopon."

Let's begin in the beginning.

1/16/17

Mania has always controlled my life, and depression has severely prevented me from life itself. Now, it is time for me to stare this demon in the eye and take it down. I want to start this journey with an exercise. First, I want you to inhale and then exhale through your mouth. Do it again. Now, do it faster then scream, "ahh" every two times. Next, do this ten times fast. Last, imagine "William Tell Overture" slowly playing while you do that. This is how my life and mind work, causing me to never flourish the way that I wanted to. There are too many ambitions, ideas and aspirations that I wanted to obtain in this life, but this problem, my struggle of my severe bipolar disorder has caused me to encounter major setbacks in my life.

Now, imagine breathing like Darth Vader slowly when you wake up and then it continues like that for the rest of the day. Then your day feels hopeless as you move like a sloth. Depression is the worst when you're bipolar because you are so far deep down on this spectrum that it is worse than being diagnosed with actual depression. Now, imagine feeling like this for nine to eleven months straight after a manic episode that recently occurred for three to five months of hearing, "William Tell Overture" in your head all of the time.

I hate waking up everyday feeling like a different person. The only person that I want to be is my best self, David. There are so many alter egos that I have when I wake up. This has destroyed me in my early adulthood, but I am tired of this stupid excuse because it isn't an excuse anymore. Ever since my diagnosis of bipolar disorder two years ago, I have made an effort to neutralize and improve my mental health everyday through shear determination, willpower, and without medication. My therapist says that I am one of few who she has seen in 20 plus years who has worked so hard with no medications to get better. But, I can't shake it at to sustain a state of equilibrium for more than a few days.

It is time to try something new because I need help. This demon is going to be destroyed, and it is time for me to take my life back so I can live with discipline, spontaneity, freedom, and the creativity in the controlled fashion that I want to.

Prescription medications are the worst. I have been diagnosed with bipolar disorder over two and a half years ago, and I have chosen to battle this demon or angel without medication. Nevertheless, it has been rough. The pills they made me take in the hospital made me feel like a normal person. Who wants to feel normal? It was disgusting. I wanted to kill myself. So, I decided not to take prescribed medications for bipolar disorder. You may have heard of Lithium and Depakote because those are mainstream bipolar disorder treatments. Those are stupid names. Do you want to hear an even dumber name, Lamictal? Yes, medication names are dumb. Let's be honest; I am going to re-brand this drug calling it "Gray Poopon," spelling it like the color and how I assumed it will make me feel, pooped on. Let's be honest, taking Lamictal is either going to make me feel like a fresh jar of Grey Poupon or like a Gray Poopon. I don't know what the answer will be to that is yet. But, this is going to be an account of my yearlong journey of taking Gray Poopon. Hopefully, by the end of the experience, I'll be on your futon spreading your girl like Grey Poupon, not feeling like a Gray Poopon. Which one of those results do you want for me?

Throughout this excursion, I want to show you how my brain works. I want to incorporate a little poem and rap lyrics that I will write after each entry in order to introduce you to the creative land mine that I have.

You will meet the many alter egos that I have created in the past 24 years of my life, that were created in my head through shear reinvention of myself.

In no particular order: Duke Lagos, Skeezy Skam, Zos, CoffeeBlack, The Cat of Cinema, David The Artist, Skolz, Samurai Jack, Zabula, The Mad Scientist, and David Zosel.

Every day, I wake up and I feel like one of these different alter egos that I have. I never feel like the one that I should feel like, myself. I want to throw all of these people away and reinvent myself to be only me.

Ugh, I can't ever go another day without starting projects like this that I will never finish. This is because I get too excited about every idea that I get in my head that spins at ten trillion miles an hour 24/7/365. This makes me feel like a loser.

As of now, I am severely depressed while I am writing this and hopefully by documenting this journey for you and I, it will be the biggest key to survival for me because if I do not write, my mind won't slow down. If my mind won't slow down, then I can't sleep, which will lead to the "Mania Monster" that ensues to my downfall.

I don't want you to compare my situation to yours, and I will never do the same to you because it isn't fair. Bipolar disorder is greatly influenced by the variability towards your acceptance, environment, community, diet, activities, and your discipline to get better.

I never want to really talk about my diagnosis and my times in the mental hospital because what is done is done.

Philosopher Phillip Hallie believes that physical wounds are not as harmful as a psychiatric wound. My manic depressive struggle in life is a hemophiliac wound that I need to cure. Hallie believes that humiliation is the worst type of pain, and having this disorder embarrasses me when I think about the past because of all of the friends that I scared away from me with my fast talking –full of life excitement that terrified my friends. I remember being able to access every point in my brain where I could remember every little detail, date, and dialogue that I have ever had with anyone. Being manic is beautiful for a person like me, but it scares others away. Another notable point that he makes is that being institutionalized is cruelty at its subtlest because accommodations are made towards the victim's problems, and that cruelty blinds us to the victim's point of view.

I don't want anyone to pity or treat me better than anyone else because kindness under the belief of Phillip Hallie is the worst kind of treatment. I don't completely understand his notion, but what I think he is trying to say is that you should not feel sorry that I couldn't get my life up and running in the way that I want, as of now. For whomever reading this to compare their struggle and or mental health condition to mine is not fair because our situations are too abstract.

Another notable thing that Hallie speaks about is how hospitality opposes the cruelty of kindness. The Good Samaritan is a great example of this. What this has to do with my life is how I must find my own hospitality that will help me thrive and survive with this disorder because this idea is about taking care of the body, nutrition, and shelter that will help me escape from institutionalized cruelty, which is my bipolar disorder. Most people don't master the basis of Maslow's hierarchy of needs, and I believe that if I can create this solid foundation, then I can really turn my life around.

The biggest point of Hallie's that I need to really emphasize is that he argues for the rejection of abstraction and the identification of appreciation for life. This is because these abstractions hide human reality, and my life, mind and soul are based off crazy delusions, abstractions, and my overall out of "touchness" with reality.

In order for me to neutralize my biggest abstraction, type I bipolar disorder, I need to reject it by defeating my gifted curse through somehow figuring out how to be present, living in reality rather then having my head in the clouds, and by living through a disciplined regiment that I must figure out by myself through the aid of Gray Poopon.

If I can do this and be successful, Hallie believes that you can identify the appreciation of life in order to live life beautifully and to the fullest of its potentials.

The most important thing to me is what is happening in the now and what my discoveries will be to get better. This is important to me to share this expedition that I am on so I can maybe help someone or bring perspective to people who do not understand others with mental disorders.

You do not have to have bipolar disorder to follow my excursion in limbo, heaven and hell. My goal is to provide a new perspective for people who do not understand others with mental health conditions so that if you are a parent or friend, you can further empathize and understand the people that suffer from things like this in their lives.

That is why I have decided to take Gray Poopon because maybe it might be what I need in order to survive and thrive with my mental health condition.

I am going to go through numerous changes in attitude, creativity, productivity and many more. It is quite exciting but yet scary as well. I cannot wait to see what is in store for me because I am ready to get my life on with this Gray Poopon.

Now, after my laundry is done, I'm going to take my first dosage at 25 milligrams of Gray Poopon.

"Pass me the pill it is time to get my documentation on. I'm Duke Lagos, give me a drink of that ale, and put your shoes on. I'm about to dunk on you like this fresh jar of Grey Poupon."

1/17/17

Anxiety sucks, period.

I wake up with extremely severe panic attacks all the time, and there is only so much that my coping strategies can do. The coping strategy is for me to change my environment, take deep breaths, go for a walk and sometimes meditate. Lastly, I wash my face to cleanse myself of all the mayhem. Maybe that is why I choose never to sleep. It is like I am afraid of seeing the Manic Monster that haunts my dreams, sort of like Freddy Krueger in the "Nightmare on Elm St." film franchise.

Anxiety and panic attacks are terrible, and no one should have to go through as many as I do. Some people have it a lot worse and I can only empathize.

Last night I was having a bad anxiety attack because my parents kept calling me about the high school drama at our restaurant while I was trying to close things down there. I don't remember if my Mom was yelling at me at all, but I freaked out at her because of the stressful situations that entail when you work at a restaurant. I've never been good at playing anything cool. Most people would play it cool in those situations, but when the bipolar monster kicks in,it will unleash the wrath upon the ones that love you the most.

Mo Tzu believes in the golden rule of how we should treat others on the basis of how we would like to be treated. I need to follow his philosophy of having a quest of becoming universally benevolent, which is a tall task in order to be a better person to not only myself but to my family and friends. Your community around you and how you treat it will determine major developments or detriments to your overall mental health.

Mo Tzu has a major impact on me with this belief, and should be applied to the methodology of treating mental health because he emphasizes that if you are not universally benevolent, then you are selfish seeking your own advantage. This quest for balance that I am on is not for me; it is for others around me to benefit towards having me be my best self.

That is going to be my approach in this Odyssey that I am on. He believes that love is the fundamental basis for living a benevolent life, and that universal love is meant where there are no distinctions made between family, friends and others. It is only through love that you can get justice, and if I can find the love in my heart to be a better person to all, then I can get justice towards my gifted curse of bipolar disorder.

At this point in my life, there is a strong disliking in my heart toward my extended family, the FR's (former relatives) that have seriously wronged me recently after my Grandfather's death. I need to figure out how to forgive them and find a bittersweet love for them, but this will be extremely difficult for me.

As I grow older, I hate yelling or freaking out at my parents. They don't deserve this at all. I try not to, but my anxiety kicks in so bad that I can't handle anything. My Mom doesn't deserve a son who yells at her when she asks simple questions, which wouldn't stress out other people. But for me, I get stressed and freak out. I hate it. I am taking this medication for my Mom and for my Dad, and I am really scared of what I'm going to turn into. But whatever it is, I hope that the monsters inside of me will disappear, and a new person will reincarnate my soul; creating whatever alter ego for myself that will stay with me forever and ever.

I want to breath differently, and I never want to hear "William Tell Overture" ever again. Fuck that song.

Bipolar disorder is a chemical imbalance, one moment I may have hypomania the next minute I am dysthymic. Those are the sub-levels of mania and depression. To put it simply there is a spectrum of different moods that you have, which sway from one end to another. In the middle would be balance or equilibrium but this doesn't stay very long with anyone with this disorder. To the far right end of the spectrum there is mania, which is not a point that you ever want to get to because it is way too much fun. In the middle of that side of the spectrum is hypomania, which is the most dangerous because you are flirting with mania and equilibrium. Hypomania can be healthy but you need to absolutely watch out for the "X" factor, which is an uncontrollable force that triggers a manic episode. To the far left of this spectrum is depression.

For anyone who suffers from bipolar disorder, depression is horrible because it is extreme,compared to anyone who suffers normal depression. When going through a depressive episode, it lasts much longer than a manic episode, and they are not fun at all. In between depression and equilibrium is something called dysthymia, which is a point of the early coming of a depressive episode. The challenge is to stay in your equilibrium phase, which has been something that I have severely struggled with during my whole life. If you sway one way, then you need to snap out of it and do the things that you need to do to get back to the middle. This is easier said than done because of the “X” factor.

Everyday in my life I have woken up and have felt like a different person. Whichever incarnation that it has been, it has lead to me realizing the continuous inconsistencies that have prevented me from achieving my overall goal; taking over the world in my own spectacular way.

That right there is a bipolar thought. I have tried everything without taking medication for this gift or curse: exercise, nutrition, therapy, competition, sleep and etc. I am hoping maybe this Gray Poopon will help me get my life on.

“My name is Duke Lagos, and this is my first time rapping, my second day taking Gray Poopon, and I just pray that we get along.”

1/18/17

Good morning. I took my Gray Poopon and I am ready to get my day on. One problem, I feel like an absolute piece of shit. My anxiety is through the roof. I have to work from 3 pm to midnight at my parent's restaurant. It is currently 10:30 am. For me, a successful day would be this:

1. Journal
2. Work on my blog (TheZosKnows.com)
3. Work on my television pilot.

4. Network on Linkedin to fulfill my career coach's assignments.
5. Fulfill my business mentor's assignments (Social media stuff).
6. Go to the gym.
7. Edit my feature-length film.
8. Watch three movies.
9. Check my email.
10. Apply for jobs.

On top of all that, I still need to go grocery shopping. I have no food.

My therapist says if you can do two to three of those things every day then it is a good day. That is supposedly what normal people do every day.

I have never felt normal. My brain races at 10 trillion miles per hour. Writing down those tasks stressed me out. In all honesty, I will get three of those things accomplished if I am lucky. But, if I prioritize according to my time, I can get these accomplished:

1. Journal
2. Fulfill my business mentor's assignments
3. Go to the gym
4. Work on my blog.
5. Check my email.
6. Maybe go to the grocery store after work.
7. Print out a hard copy of my TV pilot after work.

I am doing the first thing right now, that's a good start.

The problem is that I want to take over the world all the time. All of those ten things that I've written down are the duties in part of my diabolical plan to take over the world in my special way: Being Zos.

Out of all the alter egos that I have, "Zos" is the best. Hence, "The Zos Knows."

Real talk, I really need to go grocery shopping. It will save me a lot of money this month. But, I have so much anxiety going to the grocery store. Holy shit, I have to decide which grocery store to go to because I live by five of them. I have to budget for what I am paying for. Then I need to buy enough food for the month, so I have to strategically plan out what meals I need to eat in my head. Next, I need to eat before I go to the grocery store because we all know if I go to the grocery store hungry, I'll spend 75% more on food that I can eat in a month. Then I'll have to throw half of it away. Oh my goodness, I should totally make a list. Anyway, those are 10% of the anxious thoughts that I have in my head before going to the grocery store.

I wish my brain were like a dinosaur's where I could only focus on one thought at a time. See food,eat food. See task,complete task. You know?

I don't have anxiety problems. I know for a fact that my anxiety is at the same level as most people but adding bipolar disorder to the mix increases my level of anxiety through the roof. It's because my brain is spinning at an insurmountable rate. I really hope this Gray Poopon will spread it out. Today is day three and I feel optimistic about this. But, this is a six-month to a yearlong journey to find out what it will do to me.

Despite feeling optimistic, I feel like a piece of shit because it is now 11 o'clock. Everyday is a race against time. It is David versus the day. If I don't win the day, it means that I have lost. Every week is a 7 game NHL or NBA playoff series. You need to win 4 out of 7 days to win the week. If I can consistently win the week, I will be a winner.

So, if I wake up at 10, that means I have 12-14 hours to accomplish what I want. If I wake up earlier, I can have more time to win the day. It boils down to this; if I have more time then I am more relaxed. But, if I have less time I am more focused and my anxiety kicks in, leading me to be more focused. I am then a man on a mission, and I've worked way better under pressure. It is important that I master the art of the happy medium so that I can be at my peak performance all of the time.

That is the problem. I can't always live life under pressure. Some athletes play better in the playoffs than the regular season. Why do I always have to be in playoff mode: stressed the fuck out and under pressure.

"My name is The Zos, and this is my first-time rapping, this single is gonna drop big on the West coast. Cause I am going coast to coast like butter on toast because I am the Zos. We all know The Zos is about to get it on, gonna spread my tasks out like salads on croutons, chilling on your futon, where is my Gray Poopon? Took that shit for the third day, ready to feel my results turn on. Y'all better listen to me because I am playing the cards that life chose, so remember because The Zos Knows what's on."

1/19/17

Prologue:

My best friend says that everything stresses me out. Man, that needs to stop. Most people are not like that. All of my close friends don't have a care in the world. They float along life and everything works itself out. I need to adopt that mentality. For me, I go about life at 100 miles per hour, trying so hard, attacking every moment and I get let down, leading to serious depression. That is how my mental health shift works. It is frustrating, but I have the habitual optimism that one of my ambitions will reward me in a big way one day.

Moreover, my depression is getting worse as it is getting colder and darker in Minneapolis, and it will take a long time for this Gray Poopon to kick in as I am taking a very low dosage of 25 milligrams and thus far, I haven't seen much of a change. As you know, I am at the lowest of my lows that I have ever experienced. This is even worse than the time that I got released from the mental hospital. After I got out, it became a time where I put myself in isolation for almost a year to rediscover myself and what the imbalance in my brain was capable of. Man, that was a dark and depressing time; a year of depression that lead to five months of a hypomanic explosion.

What made this time worse was that all of those feelings that I endured over that time are all compressed in every fleeting moment of this period in the time of my life.

What has caused all of this is that the minute I get home from the most amazing sojourn in South America, my best friend broke his hip, went to the hospital and slowly died of pneumonia. That man was my Grandfather, who I took care of along with my Grandmother for the last two years when I lived with them.

I am so heartbroken and I'd give anything to talk to him again for one last time. The worst part is that super high immediately followed a major low when it happened. After he died, my extended family tried everything to kick me out of the house and replace me with another relative to take care of my Grandma. When I refer to them in my documentation of this journey, I will call all 15 of them "FR," standing for "Former Relative." Remember that because it is important to following along with my story. FR could mean my cousin, uncle, aunt or ETC.

They all ganged up on me, 15 vs. one, forced me out of my living space, separated me from my Grandma who I love so much, made up stories about me, said I was going to kill myself, said that I was going to hurt someone and that they were "concerned" about my bipolar disorder. Yes, they played the bipolar disorder card with me. No one should ever do that. That is so intolerable and unacceptable.

I tried so hard to protect my Grandmother from all of them because they never gave her time to grieve over his death. They are trying so hard to kick her out of the house and sell it, putting her in a nursing home and this is not what she wants or needs. Besides my Father, I cannot believe that none of her children, whom she brought life to, are not abiding by her wishes, with love, honor, integrity and respect for their matriarch.

This lead to my delusion, paranoia, panic attacks, anxiety attacks and my current depression. Then they really ganged up on me and played the bipolar card even stronger and harder.

This is some white people shit. My Asian side of the family would have never done this.

Growing up, I've always had an identity crisis. Imagine going to your Grandparent's house when you're four for Thanksgiving, and you become confused on why you do not look like anyone and then this goes for the same on your other side of the family. Being a mixed raced person provides many dilemmas in terms of customs, culture, identity, and a sense of belonging. In school the Asian kids never accepted me, and neither did the white kids. This is how and why I decided to become friends with everyone, creating strong individual relationships. But, with the recent chain of events that happened between my white family and I has made me realize for the first time in my life to identify myself to be Asian. This has brought major closure, relief, and has lifted a weight off my shoulders.

At this point in this entry, I need to reflect on the current pain that I have in my life, which were huge life changes for me that culminated into my breaking point that started this journey.

For me, this will be a day that I will always remember. I even know the day and times that this happened to me. It was December 17th, 2016 at 7:45 pm when the owner of the company, of whom I've been with for five years informed me that the company was under legal duress and that I was laid off. He did this to protect the business and I. It was like a divorce just happened. Five years is like marriage, man. Prior to this at 10:45 in the morning my FR's kicked me out of my Grandparents house, leaving me to the streets, crashing on one friend's piss smelling couch to another for a few weeks. I loved that job because I was pioneering a new field and I became the best at what I did, making an absurd of amounts of money that no kid from 19-24 should be earing at their first job. After I walked out of my layoff meeting, I drove to my parent's restaurant and took a job as a dishwasher at 8:45 pm. Washing those dishes that day gave me the greatest humbling experience of my life. With three major life changes, I knew that I needed to make that step to move forward and take a prescription medication. People with bipolar disorder or with mental illnesses struggle with major life changes. I will never forget that day for the rest of my life.

Needless to say, this was not the "Good Day" that Ice Cube was referring to.

What kills me the most is that I tried so hard to protect my Grandmother but I failed her. How can I protect my Mom, my Sister, and the potential woman that I love if I failed to protect my Grandma? It breaks my heart every time that I think about it. But, I need to stay sane and strong by doing one of the most difficult things ever for me, which is to not be so hard on myself.

With my mental health conditions, I only knew that I could be so strong and that I needed to take this next step to find Gray Poopon.

All bad things happen in threes, so the only way to go is up, right?

I am not asking for your sympathy but only your support in my journey. I really need support right now.

My optimism and positivity is the only thing that I have right now in this darkness of depression. Seasonal Affective Disorder is terrible for bipolar or mental health victims in these cold and dark winters here. It is my optimism that represents the candle in the dark that is a flickering as I am shivering in this cold Minnesota winter. There is a Chinese proverb that states, "It is better to hold and light a candle then to curse the darkness".

The Meat and Potatoes of this entry:

So, I know what I have to do at the grocery store to resolve that issue from my last entry. I need to buy cereal, milk, and lunch food. Keep it simple. There, my anxiety about that is cured. It is so hard for me to believe that it takes me one whole day to get over stresses of simple tasks like that. Golly, and to think it sometimes takes a lot longer.

Today is day four of taking Lamictal, aka "Gray Poopon." It is quite the tiny pill and is nothing scary thus far. The Gray Poopon dissolves in your mouth on contact with the water. It is not like any of those horse pills that they made me take in the hospital, which turned me off from prescription medication.

People have misconceptions whenever they find out someone is bipolar. The main one is that people with the disorder are viewed as violent and have crazy mood swings. Yes, I have mood swings, but mainly out of excitement and passion. I am either the happiest man in the world or the most hopeless person in the world. As I mentioned before, I have varying alter egos of who that person may be. But to make things clear, I do not have multiple personality disorder. These alter egos are simple mere characters that I have used to reinvent myself whenever I have hit major dysthymic or depressive episodes in my life to kick start optimism, creativity, and opportunity. But, I need to be careful because I need to not fall into mania.

It's easy to fall into mania and to be honest; it is so much fun. Having a manic episode is something that is hard for me to be aware of because of the "X Factor." This is when your brain spins from 10 trillion miles per hour to over 100,000 trillion miles per hour. This causes me to talk so fast where my mouth can't keep up with my brain. Then my mouth gets dry, my fingertips create cuticles and blister, I can't sleep, I can't eat, I speak a language that I only understand, and then I live in fear and paranoia that I will be in the hospital.

After my first manic episode and hospitalization, I have survived other manic episodes by doing one of two things:

1. Create a huge project to focus all of my energy into.
2. Isolating myself from people.

It took me over three months to find a new psychiatrist to get prescribed Gray Poopon. This was difficult because there is a huge shortage on psychiatrists in the world right now. They work one day a week and they also never get back to your phone calls. When they do get back to you, they always call you at the worst time. Psychiatrists also call you from different numbers, and I never answer to random numbers because I don't want some dude calling me and getting up in my business.

I could have checked myself into the hospital for depression and have experimented with bipolar medication. This is because this is the easiest way to get prescribed medication.

Instead, I decided to write about my experience with trying medication on the "outside" for every day that I take this Lamictal or as you know, "Gray Poopon."

I have created this source of energy channeling challenge for myself to overcome my bipolar disorder and distrust for medication.

Those were my two cents for today.

Epilogue:

“My name is Skeezy Skam, and this is my first time spittin beat's on this jam. You know I got this, fam. C'mon, sit back on your futon. Dawg, make me a sandwich and don't forget that Grey Poupon.”

1/24/17

Prologue:

Isolation is one of the most underrated situations in the world. Sometimes, it is good to be alone with your thoughts rather than being surrounded by mania. My short hiatus was due to the fact that I took an impromptu adventure out into the wilderness to my best mate's cottage in Luck, Wisconsin. I enjoyed my sojourn away from the town that I love. While I was away, I rode across treacherous terrain on ATV's, did some yoga, meditated, watched some football and ate some pancakes.

These pancakes were the best that I have ever had. Pancakes are one of the top five things in the world that instantaneously make me happy.

I have discovered something oddly strange about myself. My best mate, Remy Williams and I have been conversing with British accents for quite some time. The thing is whenever I speak in my "rock star" British alter ego, I lose all grip on anxiety, stress, and depression. Doing goofy things is vital to neutralizing mental health issues.

So, I got to thinking.

What if I moved to Great Britain or Australia and developed a wicked accent and then came back to the states, living in a different city like Nashville afterwards that I could speak in a British Commonwealth realm accent in.

Would that make me a phony or a reincarnation? Would that reincarnation cure my mental health issues?

I already know who I am but what if the real me doesn't fit my mental health issues? Could or should I become someone else to escape my problems right now?

My Father always told me that if you move away and find a new situation that your problems will always follow you. But, he never said anything about becoming a completely different person.

These are uncharted waters that I am approaching. Maybe I should start thinking like this alter ego that I have created. There is no name for him yet, but he seems to be so even keel: something I am not.

On top of that, I have found other forms of becoming balanced other than Gray Poopon and acting like a bloody British bloke. That would be competition. I got done playing one on one basketball with my best mate, Remy Williams, and every time we play each other I feel centered, balanced and focused.

I need to mention that I won this time around. That is not the point. Something about competition makes me feel healthy. It is too bad that I can't find a mate to do something competitive with me every day. Not everyone's schedules line up perfectly with mine.

As of now, I am really disoriented from being on this adventure, and I plan on slowly easing back into my normal life. Boy, it was a good time riding ATV's 40-50 miles per hour out on a frozen lake, drifting like it was "Tokyo Drift." Another comparison would be like a James Bond film because all you needed were some guns. I also recall being out on a few racetracks, and since it was so foggy and misty out in the wilderness, it also reminded me of being in a zombie film.

How fun would that be? Riding around on ATV's, running over zombies.

Movies are a huge part of my life. I would like to be able to watch movies all day long and share those experiences with beautiful people. It isn't really a realistic lifestyle but I think I can figure out some ways to make that happen.

I've always had a commanding presence whenever I have walked into a room, but at the same time, I am as shy and timid as the next person. Now, that was a bipolar thought.

Crazy, that this is how my brain works most of the time. Could I be a walking-talking contradiction? I need to figure out how to put an end to this.

Changing lanes, I want you to count backwards from 15. Next, read the rest of what I have to say. Are you counting? Do it. Keep counting. Five. Four. Three. Two. One. Queue the music. That is how long it takes for you to ignite the spark of the impulse to creating your addiction to streaming content.

Everything we get in today's society is instant. Instant pudding, access to the world-wide-web, messaging, knowledge, snap chats and online streaming. Human beings have slowly lost the concept to learn the virtue of working for something and obtaining a glorious result. The world is going to drive itself insane, only due to the way we as Homo sapiens have chosen to evolve in the past 20 years.

Dopamine levels in your brain have been released. Netflix is a dangerous drug because like most drugs, it is cheap, easily accessible, high quality, mixes well with other drugs but the main difference is that it is perfectly legal. You can get your fix anywhere.

I need to be saved from my mind and from my soul, so I can be a finisher in my ventures. My mind needs to slow down, and I am excited about this point in my journey because at 25 milligrams I am starting to see a slight path of clarity that is starting to crack open.

Now, this is where my point about the addiction of instantaneous belief that Netflix comes in.

This is so terrible but it is who I am. I want to take over the world. Have my own 747 Boeing private plane. Filled with champagne and models and scour the earth for the most remote desired locations. I want to look to the left and 100 million dollars falls out of the sky for me. I want a conglomerate, a record label, a production company, a best-selling book series, to own the LA Kings, an Oscar, a technological startup and apartments in many countries that are homemade by trusting people who Airbnb them out to strangers because those people want to stay where I live. But, I want it to happen now. I want this overnight and that is all that I think about. Now, I am realizing in a pragmatic way that this is not idealistic at 25 milligrams of Gray Poopon.

There is nothing wrong with having crazy and outlandish dreams, but this has been my greatest downfall because I am not realistic or strategic about them.

Instead, I am a manager at a restaurant, my parent's restaurant. I barely get by. I have an unfinished feature film, a blog with no traction, an opportunity with a television pilot that may never be anything and some credit card debt. I forgot to mention that I have a few dents on my car as well. My life is always about getting a brand new shirt and then spilling mustard on it. But, I have the strength to wash it and move on through shear determination and perseverance. The key is to be resilient.

Those were two bloody different paragraphs. I am where I am because of what goes on in my brain. I haven't been able to master my fullest potential yet, and I truly believe if I can figure out how to tame this beast inside of me and take care of myself that I can reach some form of the unrealistic idea of success that I have. If other people can accomplish those things, then why can't I?

Why can't I live my life out chasing my wildest dreams? Would life pass me by? I need something big to happen to me soon. I am tired of my brain rattling me and keeping me in limbo for so long.

I am too stupid to ever give anything up. With my current mental stability, I don't fit in at one of those 9-5 jobs. When this changes, I will be able to fit in and thrive in that environment. Right now, I need to figure out how to live a lucrative lifestyle. I don't want to be a 35-year-old alcoholic living in squalor, given up on life, thinking that I am above the norm.

Maybe, I am a 24-year-old in that same position now? But, I am not an alcoholic or a drug addict. Thank goodness for that. Like how water and oil do not mix, bipolar disorder and substances do not mix well at all.

There are many degrees of alcoholism, and I may fall under one. I do not know what that is. The types of alcoholics include the young adult alcoholics who are the social binge drinkers. Another is the young antisocial alcoholic who grew up around alcoholics and began their drinking careers at a young age; most have an anti-social or mental health disorder. Next is the functioning alcoholic, who drinks everyday and functions in society. There is also the immediate familial alcoholic and the severe alcoholic.

Could I be a young adult alcoholic? That would mean that me and all of my friends, peers, and anyone who goes out on the weekends are all alcoholics! Holy smokes.

I need to figure out how to turn the tide on this.

If I drink too much coffee, I go crazy. If I smoke weed, my anxiety level goes through the roof. If I drink alcohol, my depression skyrockets. None of that is good for me, but yet I do all of those things as recreational activities.

Gosh, I remember while at university I was constantly mixing all of those drugs including Adderall every day for four years. Most college students do all of those things, but that doesn't mean that I should have partaken in it. But, I didn't know that I was bipolar until my senior year of university. I was oblivious to it, but I can't be hard on myself because I didn't know how badly that chemicals could affect me. So, I did them anyway without knowing why it affected me so much. Once I found out my diagnosis, I cut out all of that stuff from my life because I knew it was bad for me. As I grow older, I realize that I do not need to try to keep up with all of the excesses that influences our society (drugs, alcohol, and sex).

I don't have a problem with any of those things right now, but 100% sobriety has always flirted with me to give it a try.

There are so many things to figure out in life. Seriously. What is there to know? There is nothing to know. But at the same time, there is so much that is out there that I haven't even discovered yet and I want to learn.

All I need to do is take care of myself and everything will be okay. Eat three meals, sleep eight hours and do everything that you set out to do for that day.

We have to keep on keeping on.

Epilogue:

"My name is David Zosel, and I am going global. This may be my first time rapping but it ain't my first time acting. Life is one big stage and I'm playing the Don, I'll send my crime family out on ya while I get my hoop on. Hit a triple-double, hop in my Maserati getting my cruise on and maybe I and my brain will get along like a hot dog with Gray Poopon."

1/25/17

I got drunk last night. At 25 milligrams, I don't think medication and serious amounts of alcohol mix very well because this entire day has been terrible. I was on edge and freaked out at my Father. I hate freaking out at my parents. They don't deserve it. This is a very touchy subject on both ends because I shouldn't be this horrible as a son. I love my Father, and after seeing him lose his Dad I could not imagine what life would be like without my Father. Why does he have a son that freaks out and yells at him? The other big issue is that I need to tread cautiously with taking alcohol with this medication.

In order for me to find equilibrium in my life I have to have everything rolling on all cylinders. Everything has to function well to be happy. If someone took a hammer and smashed your toe with it, then despite the rest of your body feeling normal, you still will not be happy. This is a metaphor that applies to Thomas Aquinas' philosophy of the organic common good.

Therefore, I need to figure out how to be a better son and to tame my drinking and partying habits. I need to do this fast because I am not a teenager anymore and I cannot act that way towards my parents because it is so disrespectful. In terms of what I am trying to do for my health, I need to create some balance between my youthful social life and my medication because the two do not mix with what I am trying to do.

Both will be tall tasks for me, but if I can apply Aquinas' rule for the organic common good and execute, it will be nothing but a "g-thang" baby.

"I'm a bipolar bear and a sad hopping kangaroo. Mixed up, Asian, White and true. I am a Christian, Muslim and a Jew. You ask me who I am and I say that I do not know who. I'm just bad for you, a manic depressive fool. But, I gotta keep on going so that I know who is who can be true. "

1/26/17 (Part 1)

I've been in bed all day. I feel like a piece of shit. I have to work today as a server at the restaurant. The Blonde Bartender will be working which will make the day a lot easier for me because whenever she is there my stress level goes down significantly. Ugh.

It is 1:35 and I haven't gotten out of bed. I've paid a few bills already from my phone. My phone is about to die and I don't know where my charger is. Damn.

Today is a loss, but I can turn it around because I can make some serious money tonight. Sometimes I wish I were a sexy Instagram model that travels the world and blogs about yoga or some other sort of things.

I should probably clean my room. When I do, I'll feel more accomplished and ready to finally take on the day when it hits 3pm.

My Dad thinks this medication is bad for me and likes me better without it. Little does he know that it takes forever to kick in? He doesn't understand as an owner of a restaurant how stressful it is to be a server at the level of expectation that he wants me to serve at. He says he can do all the jobs and that he is a bartender and server. I replied, "Well, what day are you going to be the bartender? Because I will visit you that day."

I'm such an asshole.

Why does my Father, the greatest man in the world have to deal with a piece of shit son who is out of touch with reality and wants to take over the world? He doesn't deserve this. Look at me I am still in bed, while both of my parents work full time jobs and run a restaurant for 18 hours a day.

I've been on other medications before you name it, Zyprexa, Ziprasidone, Mirtazapine, Lithium, Zoloft, Adderall, and Depakote. They all have to lead me to go insane or become severely depressed. If my Father has noticed me a bit more on edge while on this Gray Poopon (Lamictal) then I hope that the medication isn't the reason for it rather than the fact that I am working a high-stress job for him.

It takes months to kick in, right? I guess we will have to find out.

Alright, I got out of bed, showered, cleaned my car, and my room. Today has been salvaged.

I am determined to turning my life around despite feeling like either a piece of shit or a piece of gold depending on which way the coin flips for me everyday.

“My name is Samurai Jack, and I am ready to attack. This is my first time rapping and I'm going to swipe you with my katana. My dreams go farther than just the Americana. So, why can't I just get along, spread my life out like a jar of Gray Poopon.”

1/26/17 (Part 2)

I think my body is feeling some strange reaction to this dosage of 25 milligrams of Gray Poopon. My body isn't feeling the same. There are weird things that are putting me on edge, I am calm under weird circumstances where most wouldn't keep calm under, and I get pissed off for no reason now. This is very strange. Never have I ever felt a subtle feeling of calm like this before. It comes in waves like my body is feeling this new sensation.

Strange.

I am not sure if I like this. Hopefully, this is my body's way of letting me know that it is not used to this Gray Poopon.

For example, this slick Rick just walks into my restaurant yesterday and starts selling wine to us, trying to make a business connection during our hours of operation. Granted that is what his job description is but for some reason I just wanted to slap him across the face the entire time. This guy almost ruined my entire night at work. This wouldn’t normally grind my gears in usual circumstances.

Am I so out of touch that I don't know what it is like to be put off, annoyed, or have a funny feeling about someone?

He didn't do anything wrong. I just didn't like him for some reason. It was strange.

Carrying on, I burned myself cooking the other night while I was intoxicated which lead me to go to a pharmacy for band-aids before work. I was closer to a CVS so I decided to go there instead of the Walgreens that I am more accustomed to. While I was there I decided to get antiperspirant because no one wants to stink, right? On the other side was the beauty section and there was this guy who took a basket and started shoveling beauty products into it.

One of the workers said that he could not buy these products and it started a whole scene. The guy started playing the racism and the male card, making a huge comeuppance about the whole situation.

Yes, CVS has the right to refuse service to anyone. Yes, he was black and he was a male. But when you see someone shoveling items off the shelf with their arm into a shopping cart, I don't think they are there to buy anything.

The real question is, why does that dude need all of that beauty supplies? It doesn't make any sense.

The strange thing was that I didn't have a care in the world about it.

Then the scary part was that he came back in and started pointing a gun at the workers with his demand of needs of having the beauty supplies. While he was at one register getting what he wanted, I went up to the register about five feet away from his register and checked out with the other cashier lady. She was spooked.

I didn't have time for that. I knew that this guy didn't have any beef with me. He is just another black man who is the victim of the time. I am a POC too. Side note, for those of you who do not know what a POC is, it stands for "Person of Color." Anyway, I knew he wasn't going to mess with me. If he wanted to rob me too, he would have gotten five dollars.

You should have seen the cashier lady's reaction when she was checking me out. The look on her face was priceless.

Now I feel like an inconsiderate person because I should have not done that.

In my part, it was really stupid of me because this shows my thrill-seeking behavior and my perpetual feeling of thinking that I am untouchable or unstoppable.

How in the hell did I just nonchalantly go through life in this situation like everything was fine? Due to my delusional state of mind, I really could have put people into danger.

I don't want to come off like I am bragging because what I did was plain stupid.

I have always performed well under pressure. I think that I have discovered that high-stress situations mellow me out. Maybe that is why I always stress myself out in order for me to work better, harder, perform at the highest level and to succeed.

When I was a little kid playing sports in the basement, I remember my head spinning at a trillion miles per hour creating improbable sports situations where I would make ultimate comebacks, scoring game-winning goals, hitting a walk-off home run, catching impossible touchdown passes and ETC.

I do the same now as an adult. Figuratively dramatizing almost everything.
Creating stress for no reason in order to perform better. I need not to be so dramatic. But, crazy stuff happens to me all the time.

For example, I have had 10 serving shifts at the restaurant and they are stressful. But, I make a lot of money so there is that flip side to the coin. Here are three things that have happened to me so that you can understand the craziness of the strange energy that I somehow attract in my life.

1. A middle-aged married woman runs around the bar in front of her husband and starts to make out with me. What the hell?

2. Another middle-aged single woman on her birthday would stop at nothing to play with my long black hair and to put it up in a bun, putting chopsticks in my hair. She didn't stop at one but she put three in and then proceeded to kiss my cheek and take pictures with me.

My best friend, Remy Williams says that I always complain about being the victim. But I am not, I was probably adding fuel to that fire.

3. An older lady, she could have been retired, blacked out and almost died. I seriously saw her eyes roll back and pass out and almost fall to the ground. It was scary. I saw the whites of her eyes as a complete whole. She almost died. I almost saw a person die right in front of me.

Luckily, my Father was there who handled the situation brilliantly, subtly saving her life.

Something weird happens to me like this every day. What do I do to attract this kind of energy?

Maybe I should shave my head, dress and act like someone else.

"My name is Samurai Jack, and I gotta hit the gym to get my hoop on. Swoosh some three's, so I can get my groove on. Eat that Jimmy John's spending that cash at an Italian Nightclub. Dog, I want hot pepper's and spread that Dijon. You already know I want some Gray Poopon. "

2/3/17 (Part 1)

Goodness, I can't stand my brain sometimes. I woke up with another panic attack today. "William Tell Overture" just blasted between my ears the second that I opened my eyes. I just feel like a different person, with a different mood, temperament, and attitude. Bruce Lee is an idol of mine because of how disciplined he is, something that I have strived for everyday of my life, but waking up feeling like someone else every morning doesn't help me at all.

As much as I struggle so much to be on task and achieve my little goals everyday, I always get shit done. I do my duty. But, I am so stressed out all of the time that it drives me insane. I am 24 years old, and I should not be this stressed out. No one should feel like there are 10 elephants on top of their shoulders and 10,000 crows cawing in your brain. Man, I don't want anyone to go through the stuff in my head. The second I wake up it's like my brain starts to run like information that is being uploaded into a computer. Only if I could control it!

Damn.

Good thing that I am starting to somewhat see a change in that with the aid of this Gray Poopon.

2/3/17 (Part 2)

They say the two most stressful things in the world are:

1. Birthing children.
2. Moving.

Moving is horribly stressful, plain and simple. There is no adjective on earth better to describe moving than that. If moving is stressful, then I couldn't even possibly relate to the stress of having a child because I have never birthed a child before. I never will either, so thank the world for how amazing women are.

But, I have moved plenty of times despite not having any children and all of those times have been the same: stressful. When I moved out of my parent's house permanently a few years ago, I suffered from many panic attacks because the move was so stressful. I suffered from these attacks because of my high anxiety level and overambitious tendencies. Every time that I have moved it is like a tsunami of mania because I need to have everything moved in and settled in within that day, and I always do it all with no help. This is insanity! Why would anyone do that to themselves?

At that point in time, questions ran through my head like:

"Where is my toothbrush? "

That is all I have to say about that.

If that one thought wasn't random enough to you then multiply that by ten trillion and it will start to stress you out and you will have to put this diary down and drink a glass of wine or something.

Alcohol doesn't help bipolar disorder at all. The more you drink, the more you sink. The problem is that I love to go out and party on the weekends. It's fun to be out and meet girls and to be out with all of your mates. Even if alcohol was not in the mix, I would still go out.

More importantly, I need to be careful of smoking too much cannabis and drinking excessively while I am taking my Gray Poopon.

Substance usage can really mask the awareness you are on the bipolar scale. You may feel like you are going to take over the world, otherwise known as mania but in reality, you are actually depressed without knowing so.

After suffering an entire week of being irritable due to my body's reaction to Gray Poopon, I think my body has finally adjusted to the small dosage that I am taking right now. This has a result in fewer anxiety attacks. But, I still feel very irritable. Although it's not to the point where I snap at someone, but it is at a point where I just don't care anymore. That is how irritated I am all the time.

It's like how you have two ears. You really can't do anything because it's just there. Deal with it.

Life hands you cards and you have to just play them.

It will be interesting to hear what my Psychiatrist has to say next Thursday when I see her. She seems like a phony to me. A lot of drug dealers have more in common with her than most people think.

Let's see how 50 milligrams of Gray Poopon will treat me and how my body will react to it.

"My name is David The Artist, and I always try my hardest. This is my first time rapping and I'm dropping a number one record. Next thing I gotta do is pick and choose a girl to have sex with. Blonde one, Redhead, Black Dreads, Bedhead. Eine, Meenie, Minie moe. Catch an Instagram model by the blow. If she hollers lead her on. Spread her legs like Gray Poopon cause I know she'll want to get it on.

2/8/17

Oh wait, let me take my pill. Where is my Gray Poopon, I need to get my day going on.

Love is a complicated issue, especially with the tendencies of bipolar disorder. This is why I must tell this story and refrain from this certain affection in my life because I am nowhere near emotionally available to pursue the heart of another. Mo Tzu, who I have mentioned before believes that love is the basic motivation for anything in life. Aquinas agrees with this notion as well because he believes that everything that we do is for love. He believes that when we love, we affectionately will good towards the pursuit. As we all know or should know, love is divided into two factions, which is love for friendship and concupiscence (Lust), in which is a philosophy of Aquinas.

Mo Tzu and Aquinas are on the same page in terms of the idea that love comes from self-love. One needs to love oneself in order to love others, and this applies to me because I need to learn how to love myself in the most healthy way and become my best self before I can pursue the affection of another. As we have been told many times throughout history, we need to love people on the inside and not the outside, this philosophy comes from Aquinas and he believes that in order to do that we need to prioritize one's self being over gratification. Love of friendship is and always will be greater than the love of concupiscence

So, here is my current love story about a great muse in my life, a love of concupiscence, a love that I must refrain from ever pursuing because I am not at my best self to the reason why I must learn how to love my self in the most healthy way that I must discover.

Today is February 8th, 2017. That means it is the third day after the Super Bowl, and boy do I have a story for you.

Thank you, Tom Brady.

I remember the day I became a Tom Brady fan. It was the day he beat the Oakland Raiders. I knew that this guy was the luckiest man in the entire world and that is what I love about him. Fast-forward through my life and now it is the point where he is serving his detention time with Gisele on a private nude beach in Monaco while the Patriots are playing without him.

During week three of the NFL season, I met a girl that I'll just refer to as Lo Mein.

I noticed that she was really intensively watching the Pat's destroy the Texans.
I knew she was special. Not only that, she is beautiful. I remember thinking to myself that I wanted to kiss her. I never have thoughts like that. But could this thought lead to more? I do not know if this is realistic or if my head is in the clouds.

I tried talking to Lo Mein and I found out that she was a huge Patriots fan. The best part was finding out that she was a

Packers fan. I strongly dislike the Packers. I also met her friend Kung Pao, who was an even bigger fan of the cheese. I am a Vikings fan that despises the Packers, and I love the Pat's. This was a perfect situation to make new friends.

They didn't think so. Guy's approach these girls like clockwork at the bar. I was just another desperado at the ole saloon.

Lo Mein and Kung Pao told me that they had boyfriends. I found out that this was a very vague statement almost immediately. But, I carried on anyway and I told them that I had been pursuing a girl. It didn't matter anymore. I could have been pursuing over a trillion girls. All I wanted to do was kiss, Lo Mein. That was it and that was all.

I nodded my head and toasted to them. We went our separate ways and I thought that this was going to be it, so sayonara. A week or so later, I saw Lo Mein on Tinder so I super liked her, this definitely meant that she was single. Then I was seeing her week after week at the same place. Sometimes during odd times and days. But no matter what I'd always go and say hello to her. I have never been fake to her. She has been a person that I have been honest with every time in a very vulnerable way. This must mean something. Lo Mein has seen me in all of my phases. She grew on me I guess. Maybe I even grew on her.

My other best mate, Nigel Hemingway, says I melt into a puddle every time I see her. It's true. I have never been able to get the words out of my mouth whenever I see her. But, I am always cordial, chivalrous, respectful and positive whenever I see her and Kung Pao.

Over this time period from week three to Super Bowl Sunday. I have seen her out on dates, guys hitting on her and her phone blowing up from dudes trying to get some "Lo Mein". These guys are all assholes. I hate how she's attracted to these guys who are guys that I am nothing like. Whatever, I'm going to be myself.

Unpredictable.

I didn't even ask for her number for two months.

The three of us kept running into each other. Then the two met Nigel Hemingway and Remy Williams, my two mates from high school.

Every time I ran into Lo Mein, it was like fate had happened. I almost never want to go home knowing that I will see her again because the more we keep running into each other the more it hurts to know that she makes me feel this way.

I never bother or harass her. We just keep running into each other and genuinely always enjoy each other's company. It doesn't make sense why we don't ever go out on a date or hang out.

The other thing is that since I have known her, I have been so emotionally unavailable. I've had no time to pursue women. Don't get me wrong, I flirt around and fool around sometimes but I have been recovering from major emotional wreckage.

To be short about this, my Grandfather, my best friend, died whom I was taking care of alongside my loving Grandmother whom I was living with. My extended family kicked me out of their house leaving me out on the streets, living with numerous people in the past five months. Oh, and yes I had to get laid off from my amazing job of five years on top of all that.

I suffered a layoff and was kicked out for the second time on the same day in December.

Then there she was, Lo Mein, running up and hugging me. She had no idea. What I had gone through that day. I didn't know where my life was and I still don't.

I thought life was going to be okay if I asked her out on a date one time. The worst could be that she would say no.

Whatever.

Be a man, David. Ask her out.

So, I did. She said no. The reason was that she wasn't in a spot to see anyone.

I told her that I had nothing but love for her and that still remains today.

I got busier as time flew and grew by. We got to know each other more and fate brought us together on New Years.

She was so happy to see me and I was too. She always cures my sore eyes.

I said, "Lo Mein, I am crazy about you." Again, I am being honest. I was one beer deep and she told me that she wanted to be friends. I said that it is fine and that I have nothing but love for her because I knew and still know that I didn’t want anything but her friendship in my life. This is how I am applying Aquinas’ notion of loving thyself to be able to love another. I do not love who I am right now, so why try to pursue another at my worst self? It doesn’t make any sense according to his philosophy.

It doesn't matter how I felt at this point. She was leaving in February and I never want to see her again because I hate coming home so low. Bipolar people like me can't handle falling for someone because of the extreme lows. I've never been so low in my life before. But, fate keeps bringing me back to her, giving me the slightest taste of a middling maniacal high.

I started my Gray Poopon regiment and I have gone through many emotional changes. Irritability, excess and emotional attachment have been three big ones. Yeah, that happened since I met her as well.

Now it's Super Bowl Sunday and there she is with her number one comrade, Kung Pao. Her friend is awesome and thinks that I am a sweetheart. It all starts with Kung Pao inviting me to sit in this seat at the bar by them. The next thing you know, I am sitting with Lo Mein holding her hand, witnessing Tom Brady make the greatest comeback in Super Bowl history.

When Brady pitched the ball to White in overtime, crossing that goal line, there she was in my arms, crying. Then things got hot for a while. I've never kissed someone who kissed me back so passionately before.

Kung Pao and Remy Williams were kissing as well, creating a great celebration party.

I kissed her. Against all odd's I did. It was a great highlighting moment of my life.
Now I can't stop thinking about her and what to do next with my slight manic mindset. This was my "Breakfast Club" moment where I walked out of the bar raising my fist to the air.

Thank you, Tom.

I kissed Lo Mein and she kissed me. It was the kiss of my lifetime.
The ball is in her court now. Now, I need to start figuring out why fate keeps bringing us back together. I may never know. This kiss has gotten my mind off of my stresses, anxiety, anger and all things terrible. What I am trying to say is that I'll kiss girls but, never one like Lo Mein.

You don't find a girl like this every dynasty. You can tell that I am a little manic in my way of telling this story. In terms of reality versus mania, there are definitely girls who are better for me, but this is really getting my wheels turning right now.

Are these thoughts real, or are these emotions still a figment of my delusions? I do not know.

"My name is Bozzy Bentley, let me introduce myself as the new alter ego. This is my first time rapping and I'm about to get it on. Take Lo Mein out to coffee, buy her a salad with croutons, cuddle like a futon cause I'm the Don. Have you seen my Gray Poopon?"

2/12/17

I need to stop drinking. For 90 days. Today would be 88 days till then. I'd rather do a countdown than a count up. It'd be less stressful and more exciting that way.

Here are some things that caused this rational thinking:

1. The discipline that Tom Brady has.

2. The Lo Mein Odyssey.

3. Prescription drugs do not mix well with alcohol.

I have learned not to think too much, not care too much and to always be cool.

"ABC" is an anxiety technique that I use to stay calm. I've been doing it for years. But now I need to hone down and master this technique.

Always be cool.

Here is the thing, I blacked out the last three times that I have drank alcohol. I believe that this has something to do with my "Gray Poopon" regiment. If I am serious about getting better and progressing my life, then I need to stop drinking for about 90 days to fully see the effects of this medication. If I am drinking while I am on this medication, it is going to prevent me from achieving my overall goal: "Survive and Thrive" with bipolar disorder.

Part of this big change means that I have to either stop going out or keep going out and be the sober guy. As a social drinker, I have always been the instigator of "fun." Yes, my bipolar disorder gives me this thrill-seeking mentality to always sniff out mischief and fun. It is pretty awesome. But, I am noticing that my mood has become more stable, showing that things are slowly changing.

I still have terrible irritability but it has gotten better. Although ever since I have upped my dosage from 25 to 50 milligrams, there has been a noticeable difference in my body. I have noticed that I have gained three pounds and that I am always hungry. I feel as if this medication is relaxing my stomach to the point where I can binge eat and drink.

What disappoints me the most is that last Thursday, February ninth, I saw my psychiatrist for a follow up appointment about my medication. I told her that I had noticed that I have been drinking and eating more, which had concerned me. All she had to say was that it wasn't good to do that. She didn't make any emphasis towards why I should not be drinking or anything. No warning what so ever. Do psychiatrists know anything about mental health disorders? They are not the ones going through the mental trauma that you are currently going through and to empathize, they just simply read about this stuff in the books to become brain doctors. Albeit, it is very hard to track mental health; you can't pinpoint anything like a blood test can. It can only simply be tracked by a professional. My therapist whom I have seen for three years has been a good support system for me. The best people that can help you get through your mental disorders are people that know what you are going through. Most therapists choose that career due to their experience with mental health issues.

I told my therapist that I felt stupid telling everyone at work when I was feeling impaled from my hangover that I wasn't going to drink for 90 whole days! I honestly want to back out of it right now. But forget that, if I want to go anywhere in life; I am going to have to make some drastic changes. This is going to affect my chances with Lo Mein immensely because I doubt that I will be running into her as often as I was.

The point is that I made a public announcement, as my bipolar self would do, and now I have to hold myself accountable for it. For instance, my roommate lets call him Red Wing, brews beer and I want to try all of his cool beer. Could that be a loophole?

No.

I am on the "Gray Poopon Regiment," where I don't drink for 90 days, working out twelve times a month and further improving my life. This is a program that I am going to develop as I further discover enlightenment from mental health issues on this journey of mine.

I even found a picture of Tom Brady to put as my lock screen on my phone. This picture of him is during Super Bowl XLIX where they edged the Seahawks 28-24. He looks super determined to win in this picture. Every time I look at it, I think of my dreams, my goals and the improvements that I have to make in my life.

The reason why I bring up Lo Mein is because of the loose association that my brain has now permanently developed to think of her whenever I see Tom Brady. Hopefully, this loose association will be temporary, which I think it will because Tom Brady will always trump Lo Mein. If she sees me for the mess that I am now, what is the point in pursuing her in a serious way? I don't want to be a waste of time. But, if she did ever decide to go for me then she might be able to see that I have my life together or maybe in the future when she does,I will be emotionally ready for a relationship if it is in the cards. But, what the hell do I know? This goes for anyone for any strong start to a relationship.

I guess she is a muse and I need to keep it at that. She is nothing more or less, a fickle mistress that dangles in front of you that provides inspiration for a creative mind like the one I have, furthering me to create more literature to achieve balanced mental and physical health. Nothing will make me happier if I can master this notion and I must do it through a lot of practice. If I can be successful in finding the right process and applying it, then I can find the realistic happiness that am searching for in order for me to survive and thrive. In this, Aristotle believes that happiness is an achievement. You and I very well should know that happiness is not a feeling or emotion. When you win a football game you will be happy through that small achievement. In conclusion, Aristotle and Tom Brady are believers in the proponents of following a successfully orchestrated regimented process that will lead to happiness.

Here is one habit that I need to make a strong repetitive part of my life:

ABC. Always be cool, man.

This current documentation is an ongoing developing process that I am creating to be a winner like Tom Brady.

If Tom Brady were a modern-day philosopher, he would be a follower of Aristotle, and if that is what he is then, that is what I am too. Repetition is a main focus in the studies of Aristotle and in order for me to stay disciplined I need to take many reps to form good lifestyle habits.

I have also learned that I am a "process guy" like Tom Brady. He didn't fall out of the womb and win five Super Bowls. It was a process.

He was a late bloomer and he still hasn't even fully blossomed. That is how I feel about myself.

I have always been a slow learner, but I do learn. When I do learn, I bloom and blossom beautifully. Maybe this Gray Poopon will slowly blossom me into the enlightenment that I have been searching for.

As of now, I am more settled into my new place. I have food and my television,and computer are set up and I have all the essentials figured out in my room. I can finally start editing my feature film again. I even sold a lot of my books to a bookstore today and even picked up a drawing prompt book at the store. I am going to do a bunch of these drawing prompts every day because it is always good to do right-brained activities, to balance your mental state of mind.

Drawing is great for mental health and I am excited to get back into touch with my "David The Artist" alter ego, who was my four-year-old self that always drew.

Okay, I feel clear, accomplished and I have set a great plan to set myself up for success.

Holy shit, I am nervous as hell.

All that I need to do is stay disciplined.

"My name is David the Artist, and I am the sweetest and the tartest, gonna paint your picture and finish this conquest. That Gray Poopon has gotten my brain changing like neutrons. I gotta take this shit so I can get my life on."

2/13/17

I miss my Grandfather. Let me start out by telling everyone that I lived with him for two years and I had the honor, duty and noblesse oblige (noble obligation) to watch after him and my Grandmother. He was the knight that protected her and I was his squire. When he had passed, I had fought to the end of the earth to protect her until my time was up. When a Knight's duty is over, it is over.

I miss him so much that I moved a few blocks away from where his ashes were buried. I wanted to see the funeral pyre, but my family dismissed everything and spited me. They didn't even have one. I want to be a gentleman, a knight in shining armor like he was, but even better. My Grandfather was a chemical dependency counselor and that is the reason why I feel like I need to cool it with the drinking for 87 more days.

A month would be too easy, but 90 days is a milestone.

Well, exactly the same thing happened to Grandpa Jim when he was my age back in Wadena, Minnesota and it drove him down to run away from home as to what happened to me and my extended family this last fall. He also had to deal with alcoholism all over his family, especially with his Father.

I am not an alcoholic, but I have been socially drinking a lot more lately. If I am to take this medication process seriously, I shouldn't be drinking. The Gray Poopon is enabling me to drink more and blackout. The after effects are terrible and alcohol ruins the process, which the medicine needs to apply to my body.

Who knows I could be an alcoholic. Most alcoholics do not admit that they are until it is too late. With alcoholism, there are a lot of varying degrees of it that spur into different categories. I may be a social drinker because I never drink alone. But social drinkers find every excuse to be social by putting themselves into situations that alcohol becomes a necessity.

Honestly, if there is a game on TV, I will go to the bar. If my friends want to do something fun, we go to the bar or the clubs. If my friends want to celebrate something or hangout, there is always alcohol involved. I seek the thrills of that and that is why I drink. With my addictive personality and my extreme irrational thought's while sober, adding alcohol to that is a bad combination. Therefore, I need to stop drinking. I do not want to be a social drinker, but a tamed and controlled one. In order for me to take this medication seriously, track my progress, and see what my true results are, I need to stop drinking.

Alcohol and prescription medications are an absolute disaster and that is why I am dedicating these next 87 days of sobriety to Grandpa Jim.

I always hated drinking anyways. It is so ingrained into our culture that it is hard to avoid. Seriously, if going to a social gathering like a bar didn’t involve alcohol I would still go out and be social. Peer pressure isn’t a thing for teenagers; it follows every one all the time.

Drinking is terrible for people who are bipolar; I don't know how much more that I need to emphasize that. When you are high, it is hard to come down. The height of the fun of drinking is way shorter than the come down. That is all I have to say about that. Grandpa Jim wouldn't want me to be drinking right now.

So, I won't.

I also can't get so hung up about the muse in my life, Lo mein. I don't want her to be some girl that I drive away because my feelings are so irrational about her. The idea of her is amazing to me but she can't know my true feelings because they are the true feelings of a funky bipolar dude. I doubt she could handle them.

I need her to be a friend to me. I need to find a way to keep her in my life.

Any other thing I do right now would be too much. I need to be cool.

I want to know if my feelings are true for her in this new reality that I am very slowly discovering. For certain I think I am right about my emotions towards her but the only time can tell once I reach my enlightenment towards reality. There is a lot of contemplation going on right now in my head whether these feelings are fabricated through delusional mania, or real ones in reality. I have never had this type of contemplation before. Normally in this scenario it is either all or nothing for me. With that, at 50 milligrams of Gray Poopon, I am learning the beauty of contemplation, a new notion that I am processing. Wow, this is quite scary because Aristotle strongly believes that contemplation is the highest form of happiness.

Having feelings for someone is terrible when you are always so high and low. The best thing to do is to work on yourself and if you can do that, then there will be a silver lining, and that way you can meet better people.

I am 100% sure that there is someone out there other than Lo Mein, that is better for me and will make me better in life. This is why I can’t spill my delusional feelings to her. I am not in an emotional state to pursue physical, intimate, and or any type of emotional love.

Stay positive, David. I went to the gym today and today is day two of 12, in my 12-day challenge. So far, I have kept my discipline. With my mental capacity, it is important to stay disciplined when you are making a drastic change in your life.

I need friends in my life as support, not a romantic pursuit like Lo Mein. It is never a good idea to use a muse as comfort or an excuse to better yourself. If I ever did it would hurt me in the end. You can't put this type of expectation and pressure on people, especially muses, but most importantly your friends as well.

By the time I am on the other side of the bridge of my journey she will be gone away in Nashville, Tennessee or dating some other guy. This is why it is important to enjoy this beautiful process that I am on and to not worry about the results and or actions of others because I do not have any control over that.

Changing lanes, Charlie Chaplin is the cat that I had at my Grandparents house. He was the shit. I miss him so much. Losing my cat after being kicked out has been the subliminal icing on the cake to top things off from all the terrible things that have happened to me thus far.

Ugh, the list goes on. These emotions give me so much anxiety in my head but with this Gray Poopon, gradually I am becoming more centered and clear in my thinking. It is bittersweet because of the slight change.

I know I can overcome this and learn how to be a normal person that functions in society rather than being the fool who pretends to know what he is doing all of the time.

I am ready.

"My name is David Zosel, I run it like Tom Brady at the Super Bowl postgame show. You know I get it on when the stage is put and I get this show on. I'm like a fresh jar, gray poopon. Pass me the ball. I'm going to pass my school on. Just let me sit back eating fried rice on my futon."

2/16/17

Eighty-four day's till I can drink again. Whatever I do, I need to stay focused and disciplined about getting better. As far as I am concerned, my irritability level is starting to lower but there will come a point where the "X" factor will kick in. I can feel it.

The "X" factor is a term that I use for my delusion and out of “touchness” with reality that I’m in. It sneaks up on you whether you are depressed or manic. The "X" factor also makes you snap or freak out at people when you are annoyed or irritated regardless of the situation. It also causes mood swings and changes the level of being delusional.

These are triggers that are extremely difficult to control and pinpoint because of the delusions and how it sneaks up on you. It is one of the scariest demons to face.

My hope is that this Gray Poopon (Lamictal) will nullify this "X" factor.

Whenever I go out, people expect me to be drinking with them. The thing is that I need to be honest and say that I am taking prescription medication and I can't drink. If they ask what it is then I'll just tell them the honest truth. Being honest is something that I believe that I am at all times but being bipolar, I live in a delusional world sometimes and I accidentally stretch the truth when I don't ever mean to. I can't control it, but I will control it and that is a promise that I will upkeep forever because I will escape these delusions that I have always had. I don’t expect anyone to understand the terminology that I just created that is penned as “delusional truth telling”.

I am not a liar.

I want this Gray Poopon to make me more honest because it will help me get back into touch with reality.

Everything seems to be getting better slowly but surely. Prescription medication is not the answer to solving all of my problems. Prior to taking Gray Poopon, I made sure I would get as much sleep, exercise and the proper nutrition in order to keep me stable.

These are the three vital things to keeping the mind stable. Bipolar disorder causes you to keep the instability of these three things out of your life.

Your appetite will swing from eating all the time to nothing at all for days on end. Also, you can run off one hour of sleep or lay in bed sleeping all day long. The hardest thing is to exercise. But, if you find time to exercise for 30 minutes a day the dopamine levels in your brain will create a calming chemical reaction that temporarily slows the brain down and creates stability for the rest of the day. Exercise will also lead to more of a consistent appetite and a regular sleep schedule.

The best thing I did was get a gym membership because I used to have access to a lot of gyms for free because after all, I am the Duke of Uptown, which is another alter-ego that I have. Since I am actually paying for a gym membership now, instead of being a delusional fool, I have more of an incentive to work out. My goal is to go twelve times a month.

It is important to set goals for yourself so that you can keep yourself intact with reality.

Write your goals down. I never do this but now I am because this "real time" memoir creates a major platform for me to write my goals down. I need to stay accountable to whoever is reading this for them to know what my goals are. I have to stay true to my ideals and what I am talking about otherwise this experience will be fabricated which is something that I need to prevent.

The next thing that I have discovered is to know thy self. I know that I thrive off of competition. I have been playing one on one basketball with my mate, Remy Williams. We are both equally terrible at basketball because we grew up playing hockey. It makes a great match whenever we play each other because every game goes down to the wire. I play better defense and can shoot fade aways whereas he plays well in the paint and can shoot three-pointers. In terms of defense, he has more blocked shots but I have more steals. He is also better at rebounding than I am because I never try to rebound so I can conserve my energy level. This is something I can talk about for days because our games are completely opposite of each other that it is quite complimentary.

If I can do something competitive once or twice a week, it can center me. Through playing basketball I can come back to reality and learn about the qualities and traits that I have.

This enables me to remember that I don't like to lose and I am never out of any game. I am tough as nails and I can work through adversity quite well. These are things that I simply forget without competition.

Another thing that I know about myself is that I thrive off of creativity. I like to express myself with art, writing, films, music and much more. It can range from a variety of types through every medium of art. I can do it all. Every day I strive to do something creative. It brings out the same dopamine levels as exercising and keeps me centered. But, if I do too much of something creative then I can fall into a manic state of mind.

For example, I wrote a screenplay with three re-writes in only eight days for a feature film that I shot in three weeks. I rarely slept or ate for those eight days. Do you think I even had time to exercise? Hell, to the no.

I have been known to do this on multiple occasions. I don't even want to get into it right now because it makes me depressed. Being bipolar shows levels of immense productivity and immense procrastinating hopelessness.

I am slowly finding the inner balance to the secret of life. But, remember the secret of life is different for everyone. I also thrive off of people. You could call me a hopeless romantic.

I am a complete hedonist rather than a stoic. These are two ideals of philosophy that coincide extremely well with being bipolar. A follower of hedonism is called an Epicurean, who is a person that grabs life by the horns and wants to experience every little bit that life has to offer. That is why I am a firm believer in saying "Yes" to new situations. I want to experience as much life as possible because the only certainty about life is death.

The opposite of an Epicurean is a Stoic, a person who believes that you should rise above your own emotions and fluctuating variations of life in order to fulfill one's virtue.

My two best mates, Nigel Hemingway and Remy Williams are stoic, whereas I am an Epicurean. Throughout my friendship with these two people, I have noticed that they have found their balance for being more like me. What I am trying to say is that I have rubbed off on them a lot but what breaks my heart is that I have not fully obtained their qualities of being more stoic as much as they have from me.

I am way too emotional. If I was more stoic, I could be more centered. Philosophy is quite fascinating, I know.

Plato's allegory of the cave is a perfect example because if I were to never know about life's greatest possibilities, I would be a settler in life.

I can never settle for just being another schnook, exactly how Henry Hill said it in “Goodfellas”, and that may be my very downfall.

If I wake up in my thirties and have failed to be where I expected to be when I am in my twenties, I will be severely depressed. I had to share that because I need to hold that very thought to myself.

What I am doing now at this point in my life is a major commitment to preventing that because I want a healthy prospering life, and now I am taking the right step forward to doing so.

"Hey sweetheart, put down that shopping cart. You don't know me but if you shag me, you'll love me. You see, I am the Duke of Uptown, so hop into my Yukon, we'll roll the streets of Uptown and get our lives on, go to Greek to Me and order fries with Grey Poupon. Have sophisticated convo over a glass of Retsina, take you back to pop your neutrons so we can get it on cause I'm the Don so don't drink that Ron, we about to get the rest of our lives on."

2/18/17

It has been 8 days since I have had a drink of alcohol. There are eighty-two more days to go, meaning that there will be a lot of new things that I will be learning about myself.

When I first discovered that I had bipolar-I disorder, I did not drink for 11 months. I called those my 11 months of darkness because I had just discovered something that was very eye-opening to me. It was a time in my life where I had to rediscover myself, learning how to interact with people, attempting to live in reality rather than in my own delusions. Now with the help of Gray Poopon, this is my time of light, where I am learning how to live and prosper in the moment. So far, it has been terribly difficult but it is imperative that I learn how to do this before it is too late.

In only eight days, I have had feelings that I never really have truly processed toward reality such as sadness, depression, remorse, regret, fear and I am totally okay with it because it is so eye-opening to me. It is quite refreshing, but yet terrifying.

You can't always feel unstoppable, happy, optimistic and cheerful all the time. This is something that I feel almost every day and it is not right. But, that is what people like about me. I also like that about myself as well. It is always good to feel sad sometimes or even sad for a long time in order to remind us what true happiness is. When I was in Toronto, a musician told me, “If you are happy all the time, you won't ever appreciate it. That is why I’d rather be sad.”

This is something that bipolar people need to come to realize and deal with. When I am happy all the time, I become delusional and out of touch with reality.

This is all induced by alcohol and other substances because it prolongs your happiness, but the come down is the worse and you constantly will be chasing that high of "bipolar unstoppable prowess" over and over again.

Remember, I do not have a substance abuse problem. But, I want to make major cut backs from all vices to get better in life.

Touching on another subject about my muse Lo Mein. I have decided that if she wants to be with me, she most certainly can. I will not pursue her because I have to stay focused on the things that I am trying to accomplish. But, I want to remain friends with her and to grow our friendship because having her in my life is better than not having her in my life at all.

Behind every great man, there is a woman who is even more powerful than he is. There are so many things that I can say to her, but I just don't know how without screwing it up ever. But, there is this hope that I get from her, this feeling that she could be the woman that can save me from my craziness. But, that is a lot of pressure to put on someone. No one needs that. Plus, I need to watch myself when I say these things like that because they may be falsified feelings from delusional thoughts.

Changing lanes, 50 milligrams of Gray Poopon seems to be doing good things for me thus far, but there are major times of irritability. I hope that this is the only thing that I have to deal with rather than other side effects that I have seen such as, numbness, sleep deprivation, breaking down alcohol, shortness of breath, and loss of appetite. As of this moment, I am calm and centered and my anxiety level is down.

Traffic used to be a nightmare for me and it most certainly still is, but it will be interesting to see if this Gray Poopon can cure that nuisance for me as well.

If irritability is making me feel better thus far, I will take it. When I took Ziprasidone, I lost a lot of hair. When I took Zyprexa, I gained 15 pounds. When I took mirtazapine, I got seriously depressed off of a bloody sleeping pill. Most bouts with medication that I have had have been terrible, including Adderall. That stupid drug that is being pushed by every doctor turned me into a psychopath because of all of the focus and stimulation that it brings. It is terrible because I am not a psychopath whatsoever. Psychopath may not be the right word but it is the one that I am going to use. The drug that has caused the greatest chemical reaction for me is Zoloft. I had the greatest high for one day. I felt perfect, then when I started to come down from it, I started to freak out and have constant panic attacks which lead me to the psychiatric ward.

But, that is an irrelevant story because the past has passed.

"My name is Bozzy Bentley, I'll tell you real gently. I'm a bloke from London and I am here to cause a conundrum. Because my ambitions are so high that I don't want to come down. I just want to take you downtown like Steph Curry, a three-point sharpshooter whose really like a pawn, getting his championship game on. Shot's fired, replays on the jumbotron. I'm sitting courtside eating a hot pretzel with my Gray Poopon."

2/20/17

I am the worst son in the world and my parents are the greatest in the world. It is terrible that they have to deal with an unpredictable bipolar son who doesn't play by any rules or even acts like a normal human being. I feel remorseful for how I treat my parents whom I love very much, because of this lurking demon inside of me. It is harder to love someone than it is to hate someone. I love my parents very much and this is why I feel awful on how I snap at them because it is simply easy because of the “X” factor. I just can't stay cool; it is like I am a ticking time bomb towards them when I have anxiety attacks and manic episodes.

My Father called me yesterday asking me to cover a dishwasher shift on a Sunday because it is something that I haven't done at the restaurant yet. Instead of saying, "No, I made plans today" I just freaked out at him. I really need to apply Aquinas' rule for the organic common good, because how can we be happy if not all the spokes in our wheel are working properly. If a link in a chain breaks then it weakens all of the other links in the chain, causing it to separate. The organic common good is what I need to figure out how to apply in my life in order to be a better son, brother, friend and person.

Talking to my Father that way really makes me feel like a hammer smashed my toe, and if one part doesn't feel well then it is hard to be happy.

First of all, this is what the restaurant business is like and second, I am not eight years old anymore. So, why do I act like that to my parents? They don't deserve that. I am taking this Gray Poopon for them to show them that I can be healthy and mentally stable to follow my dreams.

I love my parents more than anything in the world. I just never show it at all. I would be nothing without them or even worse, someone that I'd hate to be.

It is very hard to come back down to earth as a manically depressed buffoon that I am. That is why this whole "90 days" of sobriety is going to be good for me. The feelings that I have right now are so meaningful and eye-opening. Honestly, I could have been a "social alcoholic". In other words, I have found ways to go out and drink. Any thrill seeking was an excuse for me.

I would never sit at home and drink myself to death. Never have I ever recalled drinking any alcoholic beverage by myself.

Today is day 79 counting down to zero with no alcoholic beverages. It is so hard not to drink and this has been the second weekend in a row. Do you know how many people come up to me and want to do a shot, buy me a beer and the number of people who like drinking around me? This is due to the fact that I am one fun person to be around. In order for me to be successful in this conquest of teetotalism, I need to apply the four rules of Aquinas' rule for the organic common good:

1. Intention.
2. Motive.
3. Objective of the act (What is done).
4. Circumstance (objective of criteria).

Yesterday was the worst because in Minneapolis, once it hits 60 degrees for the first time in the winter, people go crazy. Girls start wearing skimpier clothing, rooftops open and bars are always packed. This is a perfect formula for mania.

The level of difficulty to not drink has been insane. I want to go out, so my plan to get through this is to drive my friends around because I know all of the best places to park around town for free. Now, here is my secret to success to battle my level of alcoholism that has sidetracked me from being the conqueror of the world that I "bipolarly" have become.

I will hold an alcoholic drink in my hand the entire time that I am out and simply pretend that I am drinking it.

This is hard because I have a tendency to always drink the beverage in my hand, even if its water.

Now, I have to abide by a certain set of rules:

1. Don't fall for peer pressure.
2. Don't judge anyone.
3. Don't make any preemptive assumptions about anyone.
4. Don't be annoying around your friends because they are the reason why you are going out in the first place. I wouldn't go out by myself and not drink.
5. Don't go to bars by yourself because it will cause you to drink.

So far, I am taking this sobriety test week by week. I think it will get easier as every week goes by.

Now, I'd like to talk about the "Mad Scientist" that lives in my brain. He is the instigator of all of my life projects. Ambitions are the best thing in the world but if you have too many of them and they are unorganized, then you will get absolutely nothing done, which is the problem that I've had. I have so many unfinished projects in my life right now. They all have potential to help me advance in my life but "life" itself keeps happening to me and preventing me from being a finisher.

Aristotle's ideology of happiness through achievement does not balance with my life right now.

Here is the list of my ever-growing projects:

1. Finish my feature film.
2. Find a new job.
3. Finish my television pilot for this guy in Dallas.
4. Finish painting my friend's goalie mask.
5. Fully create a brand for my blog, TheZosKnows.com. (Merchandise, advertisements, T-shirts... ETC)
6. Start a foundation. (TBD)

7. Drop a clothing line that contradicts everything that people know.
8. Start a variety alternative website that I write about anything under the sun.
9. Write a massive article about sports vision training for this book.
10. Find music for my film, which is the reason why it hasn't been finished in over two years.

All of these things are ventures that are a work in progress. The important thing for me to figure out how to do is to simplify my life and focus on about three to five things so that I can have that sense of accomplishment to find my realistic form of happiness.

A work in progress is what I am, "WIP", is something that I remind myself every day about my process in life.

Finding a new job should be at the top of my list, but I have endured so many life changes since last September that I am surprised that I have overcome all of those things and didn't end up in the hospital again for the second time.

As soon as I lost my job, my full time job has been finding one.

Honestly, I need life to slow down a lot. I don't want any more life changes. A new job is something that brings in a major amount of change. Bipolar people hit one end of the spectrum or another whenever there are major life changes.

My extended family wanted me to freak out and go to the hospital to prove to my immediate family that I was a monster. That is all I have to say about that. They are terrible people and at this point, I cannot forgive them about anything that they did to my Grandfather and Grandmother. But, I will forgive them at one point and it is important for me to do that. Nothing is worse than having hate in your heart, and I don't want to walk around the world with that poison inside of my veins.

I tried to protect my Grandma after my Grandpa passed away and I failed her. That is something that I have to live with for the rest of my life.

But what kept me sane through all of that was my basic steps towards sanity:

1. Exercise
2. Eat three meals a day
3. Obtain eight hours of sleep
4. Trying to stay organized.
5. Seeing my therapist twice a week.

Now, I am adding and developing this Gray Poopon to my regiment and this has been quite the saga, through creating the "Gray Poopon Regiment."

I will overcome this, mark my words. This is because every day, I strive to be the best person that I can be. I want to make everyone's life better and to make the world better than I left it. I have the determination and ambition to execute this. What I have in those things, I lack in discipline and consistency. Truly, I believe if I can find balance in my life, the lopsided characteristic of those four things will be equal and I will be able to survive and thrive the way I want to.

Thus far at 50 milligrams I am on my way. This medication is helping me slowly. I just need to get rid of the "X" factor, the "Mad Scientist," anxiety, bad alcoholic habits and become more organized/disciplined while all managing to stay true to myself.

I am now reinventing myself to "keep it real" in the way of equilibrium, finding the perfect balance of mania and depression. This will equate into reinventing myself into my final incarnation of only being David, the only person that I want to be for the rest of my life, rather than waking up and feeling like a different person everyday.

"Allow me to reintroduce myself; I am the Duke of Uptown. I ain't a joker or a clown. My job is to bring people together in this very borough of my town. Born and raised in the warehouse districts of Northeast, M-P-L-S, you wouldn't have even guessed. I'll never be the "Prince" of this side that is why I am the Duke, southside till I die. My rhymes are like my Gray Poopon; you can read them on the back of Cub Food coupons on your futon eating caesar salad with croutons. I don't even know if these verses will turn into songs, I'm just spitting them to get my life on."

2/23/17

76 more days until I can have an alcoholic beverage again. Sobriety truly clears the mind. Thus far, I am more thoughtful and conscious about my actions rather than being oblivious and delusional. 50 milligrams has seriously guided me to this point.

My body is going through some changes as well due to the adjustments. I am really running down and sick right now and I believe that is how my body is reacting from not receiving its usual weekly amount of alcohol.

The only way to see the changes of Gray Poopon is if I remain sober.

I can do it. I know so.

2/24/17

Good news! I am feeling better in terms of not drinking alcohol.

Ever since I stopped drinking, I have noticed more of my natural bipolar tendencies. For instance, I am less delusional now that I can see my life is not as interesting as I can make it out to be whenever I talk to people and tell them stories.

I ain't shit.

But, this is a healthy thought. Bipolar plus booze does not equal a good idea.

Quit being such a prima donna, David! I need to shape up.

I need not to drink because I need to see if this Gray Poopon is working. It will be an interesting test to see if this prevents me from falling into serious depression. Right now is the moment to know whether this slight depression will turn into a serious one like it normally does without the medication.

As of now, I am struggling. I am sick right now and being sick doesn't make depression any better, I have always felt that illness always added depression. Who is ever happy to be sick? No one.

To make matters worse, it is cold and windy outside today.

The only thing I can do is to stay positive.

2/26/17

I figure that I am not depressed. Depression is the opposite of what I am. Simply put, I am centered and it feels strange. It is very hard to process this equilibrium. Being at the center is something that I am not used to at all due to the fact that it is sort of scary.

This realization has made me quite relieved that this Gray Poopon may be effective for me.

My conquest of teetotalism has made me really proud of myself because I need to know who I am at these times of change. I have gone 16 days without drinking, making that 74 more days till I can drink. Truly, I believe that I am allowing myself to closely monitor the changes in my mood by doing this. Alcohol is a friendly demon that disguises many emotions, feelings, and insecurities that the human being wants to avoid. Thus far, I need to use this opportunity to reinvent myself. This reinvention time in my life is extremely pivotal for myself because I can now take all of the great old qualities about myself and improve on them while disposing of old mediocre qualities of myself that I do no like. I have done this many times in my life but this one is going to be one of the more important ones.

This is not a time of darkness, which was a period I had after I got out of the hospital for being diagnosed with bipolar disorder. It is actually quite the opposite because I feel like I am finding the light that will help me combat this disorder so that I can thrive and take over the world in my own unique way.

"Take over the world" is just a term that I loosely use to describe freedom, enlightenment and good living. But, it is a huge problem that bipolar people face, including me. Then as we all know, feeling hopeless is on the other end of the earth as well.

While on Ziprasidone, I was at a centered state of mind but I felt like I was trapped there like it was purgatory. Ziprasidone is an antipsychotic pill that I took for a while and I absolutely hated it. I lost hair and I wanted to kill myself because being so centered was terrifying. When you are not used to being in the middle it is a scary thing. Especially, when you are taking a pill that is prescribed to prevent psychosis. I recall taking it at 200 milligrams right away. This may be why Gray Poopon has been more effective due to the gradual build up of the dosage.

But now, while on Gray Poopon (Lamictal) I am starting to feel that feeling of balance and it is weird. My stress level is down, I have almost little to no anxiety and I am starting to live like sort of a normal human being: slow, boring and monotonous?

Is that being normal? Weird.

Bipolar people don't like that. You know, being normal. We want to be extraordinary, grandiose, and unstoppable or we can just be quite the opposite in reality. Being normal means that we are in the middle. Which is scary for us.

Yeah, weird is the best adjective that I can use in describing it.

Also, there are other personal factors that I need to bring to attention.

I have had no time at all to process the major life changes that I have gone through since last September. First of all, my best friend died, Grandpa Jim. I have had no time to fully process his death because of the reaction of the chain of events that has caused my extended family to treat my

Grandmother very poorly. Long story short, instead of treating the matriarch of our family with honor, respect, dignity and virtue my FR's (Former Relatives) have schemed to put my Grandmother to shame; taking advantage of her vulnerable state.

You see, I lived with my Grandparents looking after them for two years and I grew very close to them. Ah man, I miss my Grandpa. I can't handle him being gone at all. It is so hard to visit my Grandma because it is scary to see her without Jim. It scares the hell out of me, man.

After he died, I was stormed out of the house forcing me to relocate twice during the winter here in Minneapolis. To make matters worse, I got laid off from a job that I had for five years. I loved that job.

I have had absolutely zero time to process the death of my Grandpa, losing my job that I loved and even gotten used to any life routine with my new living situations. No time at all.

Now that I am somewhat settled and centered, I can finally process all of those things. Due to not drinking alcohol and my Gray Poopon regiment, I am feeling true emotions about these main issues in my life. I am not depressed or sad but I could be in a few weeks. Yes, I am forecasting my mood. This is something that bipolar people need to learn how to do, especially while on medication.

Get a therapist. See him or her twice a week if you have to. I have noticed that seeing my therapist on a Saturday brings a different David Zosel than Mondays bring.

Why are they different people? Well, everyone's aura is much different on Saturdays versus a Mondays.

Moreover, it will be interesting to see how those things will set into my consciousness within the next few weeks with this medication. Hopefully, the Gray Poopon will get me out of the dysthymia/depression zone.

I am going to take the time to set goals for myself this week.

1. Resume editing.
2. Edit and write more of the television pilot.

Teetotalism has taught me that life is a process and it is a tedious one. You can't hurry and anxiously take over the world while you are lying in bed watching Netflix all day long while trying to travel to the seven-wonders of the world.

"This is Duke Lagos on the mic, taking the world by storm. That is all I have to say. Y'all been warned".

2/27/17

I think that it is well established that I am a manic-depressive monkey. It is important for me to touch on my ethnicity. Being half Asian and half Caucasian has been something that I have always struggled with. This is something that has always confused me since I was a young lad.

Other kids at school had such cool middle names like James, William or Robert but mine is Truong. I never was proud of that middle name until just a few years ago. I always wanted to be "David James" or "David Michael." I remember kids would laugh at me when they found out and I would look down on myself for who I was and where I came from.

I recall the first time I experienced major racism was when I was five years old. Some other older kid at the daycare came up to me and held a Japanese Pokemon card in my face and asked me to read it. Like what the hell, dog? I am five years old! I don't even know how to read English that well yet.

Oh and yes, at this very day care I remember trying to play with another kid and that dude said I couldn't play with him because we weren't the same color.

In middle school, I wasn't cool enough to hang out with the Asian kids or the white kids. So, I hung out with black kids and Hispanic kids. Throughout my adolescence, I never found a place where I belonged so I decided to be nice to everyone and try to befriend everyone. There was no sense in trying to be friends with people that didn't want to be friends with me at all, so why would I need to ever act or dress to impress anyone. I just have always done my own thing.

Just like being bipolar, it is a blessing and a curse in disguise to be multi-racial.

Being half Asian and white has exposed me to the gift of being open to other people, cultures, and customs. It has made me feel unique, which has always fueled my maniacal fire.

It is the gift that has always kept on giving because if someone normal feels special, well they feel special. For me, that special feeling that I have about my identity has to lead me to believe that I can do something so extraordinary in life. I want to do things that no one has ever done before. I believe this every day of my life. I don't know what that is but I want to bring people of different races, cultures, religions and ETC together.

I may be half white and half Asian but I more identify myself with being Asian and African American than a Caucasian. On the other end of the spectrum, I have been manic and I have been depressed but I have always been drawn to mania. I love being manic. It’s so much fun but you cannot be manic all the time and be successful in life.

I need to identify with being cool as a cucumber and mentally stable. This pill is slowly changing my state of mind and I am taking a liking to it.

I don't feel "Gray" or "Pooped on," I feel like a fresh jar of Grey Poupon. Well, almost.

As of now, I feel like I have kept my ambitions, creativity and my drive but the key factor is that I am coming to believe that I am living life more like a normal person. What does that even mean? Well, I have come to an understanding that life is a process and you can't fly to Mars in one day.

I picked up my latest refill today of Gray Poopon (Lamictal) and I am somewhat excited about this refill. I am anxious to know what my state of mind will be like in another month. But, I need to stay focused and complete all of my weekly goals that I write for myself every week.

You can't just rely on medication to change your life. Medication can aid you in reaching your goals but your medication can't get you to the gym, write screenplays, edit films or make you brave enough to talk to the pretty girl at the end of the bar.

Medication won't make you ambitious or do any of the dirty work for you.

"I am the Mad Scientist, and I don't need an apprentice. I got Siri on my phone, setting reminders and goals. I just learned that the best thing in life is to let it flow."

2/28/17

I may not be a millionaire. I may not be an icon. I may not be a ruler. But, for the first time in my life, I am starting to have my mental health.

It is so strange.

The past week brought me a significant amount of less stress and anxiety or depression. This means that after 43 days of my Gray Poopon regiment, I have taken 1800 milligrams of this drug and I am seeing good results.

Last week at work, I had to be the only server/bartender and on top of that, I had to open and close the restaurant. I knew that I had people there to help me and I didn't even break a sweat or stress out like the drama king that I tend to be.

I was really proud of myself.

I need to get used to this newlyfound balance in my life because it has just begun. If you have been living with a chemical imbalance in your brain for this long, equilibrium is tripping.

I am just so taken back and calm about stuff now that it shocks me that I am even capable of such things.

It is like I am Peter Parker and just discovered my newlyfound powers.

"I am Samurai Jack of Storm Born, Duke of the Lakes, breaker of rains, Father of the Wild, Commander of the Vikings and your leader. I am here to conquer the world. I am here to conquer the world. I am here to conquer the world.

The world is mine. All I need is a fresh jar of Grey Poupon to dine.

3/2/17

Ever since my diagnosis of finding out that I can be "Bat-shit" crazy, AKA bipolar I disorder, I have had to get used to processing a lot of emotions, which will take a lot of time, it is a process.

After my diagnosis I took Ziprasidone, which took me to an extreme equilibrium that it frightened me. I was so damn scared of that feeling of being a victim of a lobotomy, but I remembered that this is how normalcy and stabilization is supposed to feel from that experience. Since it was so strange to me and I had never felt that way before, it led me to have suicidal thoughts because I was processing every single emotion all at once. Due to this overwhelming situation, for the first time I was afraid of life itself.

That made me want to stop taking prescription medications for good, and I did. If that was going to lead me to suicidal thoughts then I was going to stop taking pills and take on this beast on my own.

I would never commit suicide because life is too enjoyable. There is too much that I would be missing out on if I just went on and clocked out from the game of life because some stupid pill forced me to.

But, now I am starting to feel better. No stress, no anxiety or near panic attacks ten times a day. It is like I ate some magic berry or something. I am starting to feel like a brand new man.

Here is a side bar:

CS Lewis says in his preface of his novella, *The Great Divorce*, " I do not think that all who choose wrong roads perish; but their rescue consists in being put back on the right road. A sum can be put right: but only by going back till you find the error and working it afresh from that point, never by simply going on."

Then Lewis goes on to say, "Evil can be undone, but it cannot 'develop' into good. Time does not heal it". If I've done something wrong it cannot be fixed because time has passed, I have to fix it myself. If I want to be a better person then I have to go down the right road to greatness. Last, if I were to go down the wrong road, I would have to go back and fix it. Two steps forward, one step backwards would apply to that. This is why heaven and hell can never be married; they are different essences. Heaven and hell in my case would be mania and depression, but in this case it can be married and it is called equilibrium. But, I want to call it "Phi", the golden spiral, which correlates to how symmetrical balance is perceived to be life's beauty because it is beautiful to those who view its balance.

CS Lewis wants us to know that life is full of choices and once we make those choices, we cannot go back because of the constraints of time. I cannot give up on my journey of my medication and using it to aid my self-betterment. This is because once we take a path and make a decision we shouldn't give up and go back to take the other path again. This applies to me because I need to stay strong to my self-discipline, perseverance, and commitment. The theme in this novel is that Lewis wants us to understand the ideas of salvation through the metaphors of heaven versus hell.

The bottom line is that I am happy about this slow transformation and I am not used to feeling healthy like this at all. With this Gray Poopon regiment, at my dosage level I am starting to see the light of salvation, but that light at the end of the tunnel is very far away.

When I gave up on medication before, I sunk into a major dark spot in my life because I realized what I was capable of. Knowing that you are bipolar or any mental health disorder changes everything for you if you're are conscious of it. Some people have no control of their self-aware consciousness about it because they mentally cannot. If we can be capable of this then I truly believe that is the first step in the right direction. The next step would be the acceptance of it.

But my determination kicked in when I was diagnosed, and I became hell bent on getting better because I knew that in order for me to fight this beast, I had to relearn how to do practically everything. From talking to people, eating out, handling myself in public to getting into a healthy routine. Everything had to be relearned.

This is my second renaissance phase. Right now, I have to relearn everything all over again because feeling centered is so foreign to me.

Good thing that this Grey Poopon (Lamictal) doesn't make me want to kill myself. Most importantly, I am happy that I have not consumed alcohol for 22 days now and this has helped me rediscover myself.

Handling relationships, social situations, routines, work ethic; the whole nine yards are all in the process of being relearned.

"You're like Chinese food, Lo mein. I get on up like a soul train. Down low like a U-boat. My voice is so sweet like a canary song. Open your book it is time for a read along. I feel fresh like a jar of Grey Poupon. Just got a haircut, can finally scratch my neutrons. Beat you at Nintendo 64, Tron. That's right I'm the Bozzy Bentley running marathons."

3/4/16

There have been tangles of emotional feelings today. But, the good news is that I almost feel like all the stress and distraught that I felt today were normal feelings that most people feel. I am slightly perturbed about it. This is an uneasy feeling. I believe this may be a major transitional point at the dosage that I am at.

There is a major urge to drink alcohol tonight. It is Saturday night and I am not currently waking up from a nap. This beautiful girl, named Salon Star, is urging me to come out and have drinks with her but I respectfully refuse because I need to stay strict to my Gray Poopon regiment. All temptation must be resisted and ignored.

There is a slow transformation going on with me because I am not drinking. I am seeing that I am becoming more introverted to aid my teetotalism. All I want to do is go to the gym, work and work on my projets all day. Although I would appreciate the support and love of a beautiful woman to help me along this journey, it isn't in the cards right now.

I started reading more books in order to give myself stability because reading keeps you trapped in the moment, enabling you to find a sense of balance. My aunt, who suffers from major depression and alcoholism, told my Father that in order to combat her demons she reads all of the time.

My Father has bipolar tendencies but is not bipolar. When he was in his youth, he was always known for having temper tantrums but after he met my Mother, he changed for the better. My Mother made him a better man and I have witnessed this as I have grown older. A man is only as good as the woman that he decides to do life with. Is Lo Mein a girl that I want to do life with? I don't know, probably not. But, I honestly don't want to know the answer because I can't handle heartbreak right now. Should I try to go after her as a social experiment to see how my chemical imbalances will handle it? The answer is no.

Honestly, I can barely handle feeling so healthy. A month ago if I proposed that to myself, I would have done it due to my addiction for thrill seeking. Now that I am more steady, I can make smart decisions that are not so impulsive.

At this dosage, I am seeing that I am slightly less excitable anymore about even the smallest essences. Everything that somewhat turned me on would boost my excitement that it was so unhealthy for me and vice versa. For example, if I met a great connection that would help me achieve my dreams, I would feel as if I would have the great opportunity to take over the world with this person the next day. Well, the next day or over time I would be thoroughly disappointed and I would be very spiteful over it. You could apply this concept to about anything for me. This is another realization that I have had, and I need to work on not letting my past to get me angry because it will only eat at me as I grow older. Note to self, this is one of your worst qualities, David. Fix it as soon as possible.

Since the balance of chemicals in my brain are now at a snail's pace of becoming more equal, I feel like a different grip on creativity, ambition, and bravado.

Those are probably the three words that could best define me if anyone or thing could define me.

This worries me a lot but the main thing is that I know that I have those characteristics deep within me. I now have the power to control those things for the first time in my life. It is quite liberating. Remember, feeling liberated doesn't mean that all of your problems are solved.

"I don't have any medallions but I can be your stallion because when you figure it out, life will be wildin."

3/7/17

Healthy frustration.

I had an interview today with a recruiter in the hospitality industry to help find me a job that would fit me the best. There was no right fit. During this interview, I realized that I can't work for anyone because I don't have the right experience. I am a fast learner and I have experience in literally every facet of business but I am not a master at one specific niche that can help give me the experience to solidify a job. It is frustrating being a master of none. No one can define who you are in a world that needs definition. That makes things a lot harder for the outlier that I am.

I am frustrated with life right now, so frustrated that I can write a poem about it.

"Frustration, it use to kill me but now it is healthy. Frustration, sexually, mentally and financially. I just need my big break. Keep my head up. Dribble. Fade. Shoot. Swish. Frustration. It's bliss."

Gray Poopon has helped my stress level tremendously. I am brought back to earth, knowing that I can overcome these barriers that I have. I want to say that I am grateful that I have a job that allows me to barely get by. It has been a liberating experience to learn the ropes in the restaurant industry.

Right now it is certain that I have been continually frustrated with my life since I graduated high school because my expectations about everything are insurmountable and inconceivable. Since this Gray Poopon has brought me back to earth, I have been able to realize this and come to an acceptance that I can still achieve my dreams but in an appropriate fashion.

This stuff is so real. I am furthering into adulthood, struggling with my bipolar disorder, trying to launch my career as an international man of prowess. The only thing I can control is my own health right now.

I could be making zero dollars and if I was mentally healthy, I'd be forever grateful. But, my mental health isn't quite there yet and I'm tired of being a hurdle that I keep trying to jump over.

But, I am getting closer and closer.

Back when I was younger I was a pretty damn good hockey player. I was always the best on my team until I got to high school. I played hockey frustrated for four years in high school. There was a lot that went into this but to make things short, my best friend Remy Williams reminded me that you can't play hockey well when you are holding the stick too tight because you are frustrated and that anyone in the world should know about this that it should be me. I played hockey with a chip on my shoulder and was absolutely pissed off at the world for four years. If you are frustrated, being angry isn't going to help you do things well or make your life better. You need to clear your head and keep moving forward.

Everything is a process.

Basically, I am dealing with frustration for the first time that I feel centered with my life and I am not sure how to handle it.

Do you want more truth? I am a loser, a loveable one at that. The only way I have to go is up from here. There are no limits if you are at rock bottom. This is because I am a first round draft pick who was a bust. I got to go to the best schools, meeting great people, and I messed it all up due to my mental conditions. This is not an excuse anymore. I am moving forward and becoming better.

I'm not going to sell myself short because I have ambition and high hopes for myself with the type of drive that one needs to obtain their dreams. Without those things, I'd have no hope.

Making my parents proud is important to me. I want to be the best son that there is. I feel like I am nowhere near that because I have this expectation of myself and they have their own expectations of me. I am not even proud of myself so how can I make them proud?

My whole progression of life has always been two-step forwards one step back. Forget it, I believe in myself. I am not a loser at all. I have the ability to believe in myself and that is a very powerful notion. The upside is that I at least get to go one step forward. I can be thankful for that.

The good news is that in the last week at work, whenever my parents have usually stressed me out, I didn't freak out or snap at them.

It was like my "X" factor has slowly diminished. I hope it continues to do so.

Right now, I have to relearn how to deal with every new emotion under the sun with this newly found centered state of mind. It is hard work. I feel like a baby learning how to walk for the first time. I do not know if any psychiatrist can relate to this at all.

But, treading water like this has never felt so great. I should be happy that I am going through this phase at age 24 versus 42. For people that may be going through something similar to me in any regard at an older age, be gracious that you have discovered something about yourself and you now know what you have to do to improve the quality of your life.

Let's shift gears. I am my own worst enemy.

My favorite songwriter, Frank Turner, sings the lyrics "I'm love forty down.
As the match slips away from me, I need the crowd to pray for me to turn this one around. I've worked far too hard to be this far from victory."

The only one who can defeat me is myself. I learned this at a young age when I played tennis, a sport that requires loads of mental toughness. I had all the skills in the world to beat everyone. I had an "all court" game, which meant I was skilled in all facets but I would always defeat myself on the court. It mirrors me today. A master of none, who is struggling to win the tennis match of life. One day I am going to win. Moreover, I am super hard on myself and that is always going to be my downfall.

Here is a list of things that I need to accomplish every day to call it a successful day:

1. Write 1000 words
2. Develop your next article for your blog

3. Finish your TV Pilot
4. Edit my film
5. Sell my parent's restaurant equipment
6. Read "A Game of Thrones"
7. Develop my website
8. Finish painting that goalie mask
9. Go to the gym
10. Apply for jobs
11. Promote my social media
12. Go to work
13. THE LIST GOES ON!!!!!

My therapist says that most people try to take on 2-3 of those things a day and they would call it a successful day. Slowly, I understand this idea. It is making more sense to me after taking this Gray Poopon for some time. But, I have not gotten used to this notion yet.

Joseph Pieper, a German philosopher, speaks in depth of the dilemma of work versus leisure and trying to find the balance of it. I believe he says something like, "you must rest in order to sharpen the axe for you to work harder," or something a long those lines. Nevertheless, his idea for the balance of work and leisure is something that I need to apply towards my quest towards balance in my life.

For now, all I know is that there is a lot for me to accomplish in this life. In order for me to do that, I need to get my head right and that is going to take a little bit of work every day.

"Fade away, jump shot, slam dunk. Money in the bank, money in the trunk. I ain't shit; new-found might be a chump. But, if I stick my chest out and swag it out, I might be the one. I gotta keep moving along, spread that mustard on my toast, Gray Poopon. I got the right neutrons instead of the wrong ones. While I sit here and write on my futon, I just want to say that I love you, Mom".

3/9/17

Netflix is perfect symbolism towards why humans want everything instantaneously.

The difference between a bipolar person and a stable person is that bipolar people want to be on the final step of any project or destination that they want to be at in life. Whereas a stable person will go through step one, step two and so on to get to their desired destination. With my newlyfound stability that I am barely grasping, the most important steps that I have to take are dealing with the newly discovered well-balanced emotions that I have right now.

The other day I was dealing with frustration, the last two days I have been dealing with serious anger.

My Grandfather's death back in October has seriously made me very grumpy. The good news is that with this Gray Poopon regiment, my anger level has seemed of a normal person rather than how I was acting and dealing with my anger when I wasn't on Gray Poopon.

This is a healthy form of anger that I have. It can be internalized and dealt with in a normal manner. Usually, I tell everyone what I am angry about because that is how my bipolar self-has always operated. Telling everyone what was on my mind all the time was what I did. The most entertaining person was myself. Now, I can keep things to myself and I have found patience and self-control to only talk to people that I feel comfortable with it such as my parents, close friends, and my therapist.

My extended family is at fault for my Grandfather's death. I will never forgive them, for now but I need to someday, and somehow forgive all of them and their sins. I don't know how I will do that, but I need to figure it out because it is important to me to forgive and have love in my heart for them. But, I will never forget what they did. He slightly fractured his hip last September, went to the hospital and then died of pneumonia later on. I had no control over this. But, I know for a fact that if I had the power to do the paperwork and to talk to the doctors and social workers that he would still be alive today.

I remember being there in the hospital room when my FR's, social worker, doctor, chaplain, and nurse were there. My other FR was also on the phone. This was basically an acceptance of death meeting. I was the only one in the room who looked at my Grandpa in the eyes and said to him that you don't need to listen to any of them. I told him that you don't need to accept this. My FR was on the phone listening to what was going on and she basically said that he had lived a long and glorious life and you have so many people that love you and now it is your time to go and all that jazz. What bullshit. If they all truly loved him, the FR's with the legislative power would have pulled him out of the hospital a week later and said the hell with the insurance companies policies and he would have been back at the house with his wife. If the FR's would have long gotten him the best at home care, that money could buy then, he'd be alive and well with my Grandmother. She wouldn't have to be suffering and to be taken advantage of by all of these vultures that my FR's have appeared to become.

Looking into my Grandmother's eyes breaks my heart and I can barely stand doing it anymore because it makes me so angry. But, she doesn't want me to be angry about things because she wants me to be happy. Her advice is to "offer it up" and to let it go. I have never been good at letting big things like this go.

Sidebar: Spitefulness is the worst quality that any human could have. Spitefulness is a part of me and it is awful. It is important to let things go and to have acceptance towards what happened in the past so that you can move on. This is ever so hard for me, but I am working really hard on it. I have come to terms with this and I am going to perpetually work on it right now. The greatest part about this is that I am able to do so because my mind is becoming clearer as the days pass and I am ready to take this step.

Despite my feelings toward this very troubling situation in my life, I will forgive all of them eventually. I don't know when the day will come, but it will happen. I need to stop being so spiteful and upset about the way my Grandma is being taken advantage of by all of them. For now, it bothers me every so often and when it does, it really sets me back.

I want my Grandma to be happy in the right way and for her well-being to be respected by everyone in my family.

After all, she is the matriarch.

3/13/17

During this journey of mine, I need to re-learn what emotional content is, master the ability to be centered and most importantly; the ability to express myself truthfully in the moment.

I saw Lo Mein last Friday night, along with her friend Kung Pao and my best mate, Remy Williams. I am not sure if it was a double date, but Lo Mein made it feel like it was. I have been on plenty of double dates where one couple is actually something and the other two are friends of the two that are courting one another. Whenever you are on one side or the other you have to make sure you are not trying to one-up the other couple. I played it cool and tried not to show her that I am someone who she can trust, be comfortable and honest with. If she wants to call me a friend then she can call me a friend. On the flip side of this coin, Remy Williams is growing tired of Kung Pao because he is bored. I cannot be selfish and make him go after her and waste his time to go after a girl that he is losing interest in so I can hang out with Lo Mein. This could really hurt Kung Pao and then Lo Mein could hate me if Remy Williams breaks her heart or whatever. I like hanging out with Lo Mein, being around her makes everything about life a little better. At least I may think so.

I have seen her on dates with other guys and I have seen how she has acted before. She acted like she was on a date with me. I didn't think it was a date. But whatever, I had a ton of fun that night. Last time I saw her was during the Super Bowl and that experience knocked me out of commission for almost three weeks.

Who knows if these feelings will remain in a few months when my mind gets clearer.

I can't let that happen again.

There is so much for me to ask her about and to talk to her about. I really wish I had the chance to get to know her better. Maybe she feels the same about me. Who knows?

Hearing of her endeavors in New York, studying to be an actress was remarkable. It reminds me of my time in LA studying filmmaking. I really don't know why she quit or the truth behind it yet. She is so cinematic, it would be a dream of mine to put her as a mighty queen in one of my films. But, I may have to put that dream of being a world-renown filmmaker aside. She would be the perfect person for me to talk to about this subject matter. If I wanted to be a filmmaker then I would have done so by now. I would have been hungry enough to figure out how to get it done. I will be closing this chapter in my life temporarily but, I vow to you anyone reading this that it will open again. I don't know when that will be or how big of an extent it will be but it will be satisfying when it does because I will have mastered emotional content by then.

Gray Poopon has changed me a lot since day one. I feel content about these changes and I wouldn't be able to do this without the help of Nigel Hemingway and Remy Williams alongside with my parents.

Being lazy is a huge emotional feeling and that is what I felt in the past two days. Generally when I am lazy, I beat myself up but now I haven't felt any anxiety over it. I dealt with it this weekend and enjoyed it. I didn't get any work done at all and I feel completely fine about it right now. This never happens. The main thing to remember for me is that I need to win the week.

In other news, I have noticed a slight side effect of this Gray Poopon because I am starting to break out, having a slight bit more of acne than I am used to. There are a few more red blemishes with no puss all over my back. It is sort of annoying.

Sobriety has been good as well. I have not been a drunken fool for I believe 31 days. Lo Mein has seen me during all states of my foolishness from sober to piss drunk. More importantly, I have seen her during every important life change in my life since meeting her.

My FR died last Thursday and I saw Lo Mein the day after. She continues to coincidentally keep showing up, letting me know that there is hope and that things will get better. It is like she is my guardian angel. I don't want to ruin that.

The death of my FR has left me stoic. As a young lad, I was close to him and I was always fascinated by him and used to think he was a cool guy. But, do you know what? Being cool isn't cool. He died a bitter angry man. He destroyed every good thought and feeling that I had about him before and after my Grandfather died. This is a man who threatened me, bullied me and treated me with disrespect all in a span of three weeks. Those are three things that I do not tolerate from anyone. Albeit, I may have rubbed him the wrong way by happenstance, I did apologize to him before he passed away. He never apologized to me for what he did. You don't threaten your own family members for your own personal gain and try to bring them down. He was a man who could never tell the truth, he always tried to bring people down with him for his own gain and he was self-centered; always talking and thinking about himself.

The issue of him dying in the past few months has been really hard for me. I tried really hard to write a letter to him telling him that I have forgiven him and to tell him ten things that he did for me in my life to find peace. That list shrank to five, then to three then to one and then zero. What he did will never be forgiven.

But one day, I have to do this.

The regiment of Gray Poopon has helped me defeat the demon of my FR and has helped me come to peace with it. I truly feel that without taking Gray Poopon, I would be a total basket case right now. But, I stand clear and calm about it. It has helped me figure out what he did for me and they are three things that are really positive in my life that he has done for me.

1. I want to be nothing like him.
2. I never want to threaten or hurt anyone.
3. I want to be a good person who tells the truth and does the right thing with love, honor and integrity.

I do not think that is a list of things that someone wants to hear on their deathbed.

The underlying issue is my Grandmother. She lost her first son and the love of her life within six months. She also lost me and gained a circus act full of manipulation and jesters that have deceived her. Since my dismay of my FR has left me emotionless, I have no need to be at his funeral or his wake. But, I want to be there for my Grandmother and it keeps getting harder and harder. I need to see her on Friday this week and to bring her flowers. I'd see her everyday if I could but, the circumstances are hard for me to wrap my mind around to deal with.

My FR's death has opened my eyes. Cancer is a real thing. Cancer kills people. I am thankful for my disease because it is peanuts compared to what he has had to go through. I don't want to wish bad thoughts upon him. I want him to be happy in the next life and I hope my other FR is doing okay (FR's kid). Cancer is real now to me because it has affected my family. I now know that I am coming back to earth for the first time in my life in a completely healthy way. Prior to this, in my bipolar mind, when I was so out of touch for all of these years, I thought that cancer was a thing that killed people but I never knew anyone who had died of cancer. Now, that I know that it is a real thing, I couldn't imagine if this were to happen to my Mother or Father. I would be nothing without them. They are getting older in life now and every time I see them, I feel blessed that they are still in my life. My Father is the best Dad in the world and my Mother is the most remarkable woman to ever roam the earth.

I couldn't imagine how my other FR feels because his older brother and Father passed away all in one year. He was in charge of a lot of paperwork and care for the both of them. He failed. My Mom has been in charge of four people's lives, saving them all and prolonging all of their lives. So, I don't understand why my FR couldn't save my Grandfather and my other FR. Someday I will forgive him, but not today or anytime soon. My Mom would have saved them but it wasn't up to her. She had no jurisdiction or control over it.

I have prayed everyday, to whichever God that I believe in for good health towards my parents and I am blessed that I have them in my life as I am slowly trying to find faith in my life as well.

The new chapter in my life looks bright because I have found my head to balance upon my head for its first inauguration. I am surviving and now I feel like I am going to thrive.

My film will be finished one day and I will use it to promote myself as a man of the world, saying that I am a true filmmaker through my amateur effort. But, for now I will pursue my life as a writer. One who works and lives an honest life and makes an honest living, but one who pursues his passion in his downtime. Over time, I plan on having numerous works.

Without Gray Poopon, I don't think I would have come to this realization. First I had to learn how to deal with the demon of bipolar disorder and to learn that it was a gift without any drugs. It took me two years to fully learn about what I am and what I am capable of. Now, I have to discover what it is like being back on earth as a human rather than having an insane "God" complex that accomplished nothing for me.

I am human and I am proud. The color of my blood bleeds the same as everyone else's. I will never trade this problem for any other in the world. Emotional content is the key to finding success as a bipolar victim or anyone who is a victim of self-inflicted emotional pain. I have taken a vow of exercise, healthy diet, sleep, sobriety and most importantly determination. I will find a job and continue my quest as an adult. This is my struggle that I am telling. I will defeat my struggle and thrive in life the way I should be thriving.

No matter what happens in life, you cannot have a bad attitude. The worst disability in life is having a bad attitude. This is my strongest attribute but now, I can control it. But now I must hone this skill to get me to the next level.
I have come to have closure with my FR's death and that is why I will not go to his wake or funeral. If I hadn't come to closure then I would be there. I have not come to closure with my Grandfather's death. I'd give anything to talk to him again and to see the smile, joy and excitement on my Grandfather's face again when he was around.

Life is a process and I might be lagging a bit behind. I should have gotten a big boy job out of college instead of working for this startup, got a place on my own, benefits and did the whole 9-5 thing. Then proceed to work for 50 years doing something that I hate. But, my inability to live on this planet with everyone else has set me back. My head is finally out of the clouds and I am figuring things out. I am dealing with emotions the way a normal person deals with it. Emotional content is something that I was never ready for until as of late. I have always been very emotional because they have always fluctuated and sporadically blurted out with no control. I would do the motions without honestly expressing myself.

Every emotion we have can be controlled and thought out. For example, I would be happy or sad or angry for the sake of it, not by truly expressing myself through it, as I am slowly discovering right now.

Last week, I dealt with frustration, anger, being content, pure happiness and laziness by expressing myself through control and honesty.

It was a beautiful moment of realization dealing with five major emotions in the right way for the first time.

I am not going to do things for the sake of it anymore. Expressing myself has always been easy, but it has always been difficult to control it and to be honest because I have always been all over the place. Having control is special. Without Gray Poopon, I'd be writing much differently upon my experiences.

For now, I need to keep on at it. Play the cards that I am dealt every day. Pray for my Grandmother and solve my conflict with her and my family. Most importantly, I need to keep striving to become a better person in order to find the light in this life for myself. If I continue to do the small things that I am doing, then I know I will overcome.

"I see the bee's on my knees in the trees when the wind is at a breeze, she brings me down to my knees, standing there with flowers in her hair. She brings a feeling that I cannot bare. I wouldn't think I wouldn't dare. I have nothing but love for her that I can share. The pain that has been brought upon, has been healed ever so slightly by this fresh jar of Gray Poopon."

3/15/17

It is important to find and build your community of people who you can trust and feel comfortable with. When I was first diagnosed with bipolar disorder, I had lost a lot of friends because I scared the crap out of a lot of them, because they didn't know how to handle a person going through what I went through. I remember being so alone after that and lacking any community at all. You do need to forgive all the people who have left you behind after your diagnosis of whichever mental illness or addictions you may have. It is not up to them to understand what goes through your head or what you are going through. The only person who is responsible for you is yourself. Never ever, and I mean ever, expect anyone to understand bipolar disorder who does not have it. There will be things that people will understand, but that will only be so much.

Hence, it turns out that my best weapon against bipolar disorder is to find acceptance through being open to others about it. This is no easy task. I have hit my highs and my lowest of lows. Being the "wild card" that I am, there are many versions of myself that people have to deal with.

It is important for me to thank my friends who have stuck through it all with me, dealing with every type of mood swing that I have, every emotional moment, type of face, seeing me when I am most vulnerable or comfortable. There have been very few, but these are the ones that have gotten me through my phases. I have thousands of acquaintances but very few true friends. I love all people but if I didn't have my close friends or family to deal with my craziness then life would be pretty rough.

My friends and family that have spent time with not so fun versions of myself, they have been more than willing to listen to my drama, and that has meant everything to me. Most importantly, they have never let me feel like a burden or an attention seeker.

I can't say "Thank You" enough.

My new center of reality due to my Gray Poopon regiment is starting to sink in. I don't really know if this is how my brain is going to handle the world from now on. It seems to be going somewhat well. I know that my support system doesn't care either way. They have proven themselves despite my own doubts and uncertainties, and I guess that is why today, whether this anxiety is finite or infinite, I feel alright about the future in terms of my mental health.

Build your own community, it is vital to surviving and thriving any mental health issues or addictions.

It takes a long time to build the right community. You cannot achieve this right away unless you already have it to which you are very blessed. Don't get frustrated if it takes forever. It took me nearly two years to figure out the right balance of people to hang out with and to know who the right people are in my life.

Creating a support group is a key thing for anyone to be successful mentally and physically. Albeit, these people don't always need to know about your mental health issues, you need to build your "Friends" sitcom show and base it around you and your life. There are five people in the sitcom, "Friends", so start by building a community of five people that you see regularly and spend time with. Don't get ahead of yourself. These select people do not need to all be friends with each other. I have five friends right now that I hang out with and only two of the five hang out with each other.

These people are your rocks like in the show, "Friends", hence bringing forth a sense of community of people who can deal with you, making comfort in being yourself around.

I want to talk about vulnerability.

Manic episodes, depression, anxiety, panic attacks and ETC. are not signs of weakness. It simply means that you have tried to stay strong and hold everything inside for so long. After a while, all of the pressure is going to make you pop. One in three people go through this sort of thing in life and I think that it is important to be honest about it. This is because if you can be honest with your friends and family about what goes on mentally for you, then it will be much easier for you to be yourself around people. You don't have to come out and say those things but you can be honest when the time is right to talk about it with someone else.

Most importantly, be open with your therapist. You learn how to be truly honest with someone after seeing a therapist for a while. Use your therapist as someone who you tell all of your issues to before you tell your friends. Why? Well, your friends are your friends. That is why. A therapist is a trained professional that can listen and give advice that can help you figure out dilemmas from an outside person's perspective, which is the best part. Your friends and family are too closely associated with you to be the first support net.

Moreover, I am a vulnerable person to breakdowns, burning out, snapping and any sort of freak out. When I was in elementary school, I was called a "spaz". At age 21, I found out why the one reason for this is because I am bipolar. Most people can't recover from this type of trauma because the disease controls them rather than the other way around.

I am vulnerable to other people because I am naive. Those are two of my biggest weaknesses and being bipolar is not one of my weaknesses. My parents are super protective of me and they want to set me up for success real badly. They will stop at nothing and go out of their way to do it and now since my brain is completely rewired, I can finally listen to them.

I am making less careless mistakes and can see when people are trying to take advantage of and manipulate me. It's as if I am living in a different world. This world is the actual world that everyone else lives in and it is crazy how slow it is compared to the place that it used to be before.

The best part is that I am ready to listen to my parents and fully take on their advice. I want them to be proud of me. But, deep down somewhere I still want to be the "greatest of all time". Well, at something.

But importantly, I am ready to listen to my parents.

Gray Poopon has given me the ability to be a better listener. I have always been able to hear people but it always has been hard to listen to people. I am shocked in terms of my self-awareness in the world right now. Being a better listener has stemmed from becoming more patient and aware of other people's needs rather than only focusing on my own because I am all calmed down for the first time in my life.

Being mindful is a big step in the right direction of where I want to go in life. This is a huge life change.

These emotional adjustments are happening every day for me.

Being nervous, content, honest, dealing with confrontation and trust are new emotions and state of minds that I am dealing with lately. This is the first time that I recall ever being so clear and fresh in my mind about these issues. Normally, there is a ping-pong ball rattling around in my brain at a trillion miles per hour whenever these things come up in my life. Now, I can go ahead and be honest or control my nerves.

Slowly but surely, I am channeling my frustration to turning it into positive energy. My brain is being rewired and reprogramed, making my life a lot more manageable.

The difference is amazing.

If I can emphasize anything enough, Gray Poopon has helped me learn the importance of pacing and doing one thing at a time. I have twelve to a million projects to do every day. I used to go nuts over these things. Hell, it took me 10 years to brush my teeth without feeling stressed out. Do you know how nice it is to brush my teeth? It is so relaxing. I now brush my teeth over four times a day!

Wow, major issues that I had.

Now, the next step is to execute life in an effective way with my newlyfound abilities. It will take time and practice like anything else. But, I now have this new great power and it is my responsibility to master this gift so that I can not only survive, but thrive in this crazy world.

"The world is my Pearl, my name ain't Earl. Just know that I'm ready to do everything thorough. But, first I need to get my pho soup on, then I am going to take some of that Gray Poopon so I can realign my neutron's. Pass Remy Williams the ball, get yo hoop on. Come on, I ain't the Don. I am Duke

Lagos of Uptown. Writing that shit that ain't a motto but for the clowns. Heath Ledger knows all about the good sounds."

3/24/17

There is this guy that frequents my restaurant, his name is Friday The 13th, and he is my favorite regular. What he do for a living are that he buys, trades and sells stocks for pharmaceutical companies that sell major medications. What a cool way to make a living, right? Well, I told him all about my Gray Poopon regiment and that it was the reason why I am taking a turn for sobriety. He then later informed me how Gray Poopon works with alcohol.

You basically cannot drink loads of alcohol and get inebriated because it is terrible for you. The reason for this is that he explained that one of the side effects of Gray Poopon is how it masks and shuts down the enzymes in your liver that break down alcohol. Due to your enzymes being masked, your body will break down alcohol at half of its pace and maybe even slower. This is why I would wake up terribly drunk and remained drunk for about 15-20 hours at a time whenever I drank. This is an alcoholic's haven.

Mixing alcohol and heavy prescriptions go together like lamb and tuna fish. Yeah, they don't go together at all.

It is good to know that I have kicked my social alcoholism habits. Being sober and going out is weird. Dealing with drunk people with elbow to elbow room, dramatic drunk girls, being a free Uber driver for my friends and taking things in soberly is crazy. Why don't I stay home? Well, I like to see and be seen. Making my "celebrity" appearance.

I have developed a new trick to getting through the night. What I will do is buy a beer and hold it in my hand. Once

Nigel Hemingway or Remy Williams is done with their drink, then I'll tell them that we should go get more drinks. I hand them my beer that I previously bought, then they drink it. Then we rinse lather and repeat that process.

Therefore, it looks like I am drinking.

How do you manage to avoid taking shots, you might ask? Well, if some guy buys you shots, then you fake take them. So, I put it up to my mouth and when the other person looks away you turn your cheek to them and throw the liquor to the side of your head. You need to be fast and have an amazing slight of hand like a magician does. Trust me, this works all the time. I survived many college initiation parties by doing this.

The other day at work, I had to deal with one of our most stressful bartenders. She had a lot of complaints about things and usually, I naturally tune her out like I do with ninety percent of people. But, I found myself listening to her for some reason. I have noticed that my listening capabilities have grown dramatically. Listening to people is something that I can do now. Things actually stick in my brain after hearing someone talk. This is all at 50 milligrams, wow, what a difference.

I have never been so present in conversations with people before. It is amazing. This is a skill that I have wanted to have and tried to develop since my diagnosis. Now, I need to hold onto this feeling and perfect this new skill of mine. I desperately want to be a great listener because my Grandfather was the best listener.

In astronomy a nebula is a "big fuzzy" thing in space. An interstellar cloud of dust made up of an assortment of ionized gasses and an array of periodical elements, from earth through a telescope, they are always seen outside of our solar system. Nebulas are not clearly visible objects in space like a star or planet is. My mind has always been a big fuzzy thing in space that is out of our solar system, not a star. This astronomical analogy that I am making strikes towards me because I have been all over the place, big, fuzzy, and out there like a nebula cloud in our galaxy. Hence why it is very difficult for me to be present with people 90% of the time. Right now, I am working hard to be a star, and in order for me to become that, I need to be a better listener.

Before, in any conversation, my mind used to be 100 miles away from the conversation, predicting what outfit that the other person was going to where 100 days from that point. Now, I can be so present and with it. It is spectacular.

This has allowed me to take in more energy and emotions and further empathize with people.

My ongoing list of never-ending tasks to finish, don't stress me out nearly as much anymore. I am finally understanding to do things in moderation rather than sitting for twelve hours trying to do a huge project. I remember in college and high school; I would sit and do all of my homework for the week in one day over the course of 6-8 hours in one sitting. It wouldn't have taken me as long because I thought I had ADHD back then. I was constantly distracted by everything. That lead me to take Adderall.

Sidenote: Adderall and bipolar disorder do not mix at all. It nearly turned me into a psychopath because it led to my psychosis on several occasions.

Anyway, I never could do my homework day-to-day. I would do it all in one day and study for exams the rest of the days. I was constantly planning ahead and trying to be prepared for the worst, not only in school but in life as well.

Now, I try to imagine how much better of a student I would have been if I'd done things in moderation. I got all A's in my academic career with an occasional C here and there. But, I would have been able to grasp more and take things in better. I would have been able to be a better listener to my professors and teachers all if I was taking the right medication during my time in academia.

But, I cannot use bipolar disorder as an excuse. This is not a crutch for my lack of success towards my ambitions in life. I have a gifted curse and right now, I am learning how to work it.

It is imperative for me to announce that my level of concentration has significantly increased. I would have been able to study so much better in school and pay attention better. With this Gray Poopon, I am now able to accomplish all of my writing tasks every day along with my job applications and emails. Basically, any daily tasks that I have to do with my computer.

My mind is fresh and clear. I am becoming more balanced with the world and I am living in reality.

I have found that whenever you are anxious, you are always thinking about the future. When you are depressed you are constantly thinking about the past. This is a philosophy by Lao Tzu by the way. I did not come up with that. But, when you are even keel, balanced, and calm, you are in the moment. The moment is where I am. I believe that Gray Poopon has helped me significantly to achieve this, but I have done many other things to fully utilize this drug which I have talked about.

But, summer is coming. Summer is the worst time of the year for me. The sun is out, girls are wearing their sundresses and the beer is cold. That is a dangerous combination for me. My sobriety ends on June 11th. My friends are eagerly waiting for me to get drunk with them and to instigate some trouble. But, I don't know where I'll be when I cross that bridge. Hopefully I will be in the right place. What I am most concerned about is my job right now. The past three summers have been an uphill battle for me because I have had a manic episode and bouts of hypomania each summer. Only one of those three summers defeated me and that lead to my diagnosis. But, the true test of this Gray Poopon will happen during the summer time at work.

"Winter is coming," is a perpetual saying in Game of Thrones because winter in that world is so mystical and dangerous. Summer for me is the most dangerous time of year.

I fear that I will lose myself and end up in the hospital again. This is especially because my parents own the restaurant. This is the most stressful industry to work in and run a business already, and I have very intense parents and they can stress me out a lot. Add that plus summertime mania.

It could be a lethal combination. I need to mentally prepare myself for summer and continue all of my new healthy lifestyle that compliments my Gray Poopon regiment.

Winter is easy for me. It is a time that I am prone to falling into major depression and thanks to the help of Remy Williams and Nigel Hemingway, alongside the aid of Gray Poopon I have defeated depression for the second winter in a row. Walking around during the winter and dealing with depression is like being Darth Vader who has no powers that is wearing another respirator. Depression is a little bit easier to defeat for me but mania is a whole other animal that likes to come out during the summer time.

Generally, mania lasts for about 3-5 months on average for most manic depressive people. This leads to depressive episodes that generally last 6-9 months. I have noticed this cycle in the past three years and this is a proven fact as well.

Mania is very fun, but it isn't fun for the people around you who do not understand you. If it were up to me, I'd be manic all the time. But that is not how the world works.

I have recently found the advantage to being even keel and it has made me a lot happier. Being manic leads to great levels of productivity but then you crash and it leads to hopelessness and no willingness to do anything. Being centered has been enlightening because now I can finally see a straight path in life versus feeling unstoppable then feeling stoppable; going back and forth over and over again. That is no way to live life.

What is most important to me is how I can channel the power of mania towards something productive and useful in life. I don't want this Gray Poopon to take away from my creativity, innovative ability and my dynamic personality. All I want to have is a more even keel state of mind.

Sidebar, I want to touch on art. Nature is a big part of Chinese art because they believed that nature connects heaven and the earth. Religion is also an important part of Chinese art as well because of how the concepts of Buddhism, Daoism and Confucianism are used to emphasize and promote their beliefs. Calligraphy is one of the most unique characteristics of Chinese art because artists would incorporate poetry into their paintings to further express themselves. The created polymerization of these philosophies expresses balance, wisdom, enlightenment, and the beauty of life that beholds.

I am slowly figuring out how to harness this new take on life. It is quite refreshing, but I will not be able to master it all in one day. It takes moderation and determination for me to apply this artistic Chinese approach to life, and I am starting that right now.

Hopefully, summertime will be a breeze.

"Everything I do is going to be fine. Life is not a test of time. I just want to sit back with you, share some lo mein and down a bottle of summer wine."

3/25/17

I remember an advertisement for the film, "Straight Outta Compton," and it said that Dr. Dre was the genius, Ice Cube was the poet, and Easy-E was the hustler.

The film was basically a small biopic of Easy-E's life, about his rise as one of the most important and pivotal hip hop figures of all time to his eventual downfall and death. At his height of his success, he lived in excess, partied, fathered many children with different women and lived the fairytale hip-hop life.

On the flip side of this coin, Ice Cube wrote himself out of poverty. He found the right woman to marry and raise a family with. Ice Cube made really smart career choices and business decisions.

Prior to taking Gray Poopon, I definitely wanted to live a life of the hip-hop fairytale. I wanted to be able to start any project and have it turn to gold, making millions of dollars, accumulating wealth and power. I wanted to have that 747 luxury Boeing jet plane filled with perfect ten models. I wanted to be able to fly out any girl that I had a crush on to meet me in my penthouse suite that overlooked the Eiffel Tower in Paris.

You get the point. My life expectations were grandiose and unrealistic.

Gray Poopon has started to ground me. I am on earth for the first time and I am reborn. Why would I want to be like Easy E, Jim Morrison, Kurt Cobain, ETC? These are all people who rose to success way to quickly, became icons then crashed and burned. Their lives spiraled downwards.

I get it now. I'd rather be like Ice Cube because he played it cool. He was smart and did the right things in life to be successful. Ice Cube is cool as ice, which is something that I am trying to be more like.

People have told me that I am at my best whenever I am chill, which shocks me because I have never felt cool or chill. Even if I have, I don't feel comfortable being a chill dude. It was a boring thing to me. I hate being bored; it is so repulsive to me. But, now I am finding the joy in being a chill guy. I haven't mastered it yet, there is a long way to go but I am finding solace in it now.

Ice Cube has had a long and relevant career, filled with success and respect. His legacy will last forever and Easy E will be a footnote in hip-hop history. Without this movie, his legacy would have been a footnote. Who knows? Only time can tell.

I get it now. Go and find a job, David. Pursue your passions after work. Slowly chip away at becoming a success every single day.

I need to find a good job that helps support my passion for writing, creativity, and entrepreneurial spirit. This job needs to help me hone my writing abilities. Basically, a big boy adult job.

I can't believe how aloof and out of touch with reality that I used to be, wow. This has been my case throughout my whole life. If I were to have been in touch with the world my whole life, everything would have been so different. It only took me 24 years to start figuring out the ability to be present in reality.

Everything would have been so different. Athletically I was very skilled at tennis, hockey, and baseball. I remember beating top-ranked players in tennis and then losing to scrubs because I would mentally beat myself up out on the court. In hockey, I would have gone a lot further in my career if I were more even-tempered. In baseball, I would get off to a hot start to every season then I would tank at the end of the season. But, when pressure situations always came up, I'd always come through. All of these correlate to the ups and downs in my mood growing up.

If I had the ability to be straight and narrow then, I would have found a lot more success in sports than I had. But, now it all makes sense to me how I either thrived in athletics or struggled. It was either bat .500 or bat .200. I had major point streaks in hockey or I had droughts in points and became minus five. I'd either destroy people in tennis or lose in super close matches. There was no middle ground.

Once again, I need to break this stupid habit of using bipolar disorder as an excuse.

The same goes with school. I basically was either an A or a C student. For all of the A's that I'd work hard to get, there would always be one C that I'd have to fight tooth and nail for. The same applies to women because it's either I am super successful in my pursuit of affections or I haven't received a text message from a girl in over 3 months. Same with any of my friends, it's either I hang out with all of them or two of them. Sometimes I don't see any of my friends at all.

Basically, I could have been way better at almost everything in my development as a child, adolescence, and adulthood if I had equilibrium in my life. But now, it is the time to really get my life started, now that I have this disability somewhat figured out. Albeit, this is the first step of my journey to survive and thrive with bipolar disorder.

Things make sense to me now.

The whole idea of me taking over the world is slowly going away. I can put things into perspective now. You don't want to be like Easy E. Life isn't like a hip hop music video where you can hop on a private jet whenever you want and fly to some remote island and party with girls in bikinis. Music videos last 3-4 minutes and can be rewound and played over and over again. There is no certainty about that. Life is lived day by day, one moment at a time and the only thing certain about life is death. What you do between that time is up to you and what kind of legacy you want to create for yourself.

Now, I have to face reality for the first time in my life. My head isn't in the clouds anymore. I can't let Gray Poopon take all of the credit for this because it is just the beginning for me.

Medication is only a helpful tool to making you better because it is only 10% of it. The other 90% is up to you.

My Grandfather was one of the most aloof and out of touch people ever and so was my FR. Things have been so clear to me ever since the both of them had passed away in the last seven months. Their presence and energy that have left this planet have helped me see things straight. It was like an ancient ritual, offering two human lives to make one better like in Game of Thrones or in any ancient culture. Do you know what I mean?

When important people die in your life it is a wake-up call to go do something drastic, pursue your dreams, make life changes and etc. But, for me, their deaths have brought clarity to me. I don't want to chase this unrealistic dream of being a world-renowned filmmaker, entrepreneur, ambassador, icon, billionaire extraordinaire.

I don't want to be anything like my Grandpa or my Uncle. I need to stay right where I am and be the best David Zosel that I can be. One day at a time. Most importantly, one task at a time.

I need to be like Ice Cube, not like Easy E.

My dream is to find balance so I can conquer this gifted curse. This is the most realistic dream that I have ever had in my life.

3/26/17

There are three types of people who are born in this world. People who are born with no problems then later inherit them. Following that would be people who are born with many problems and must later solve them. Then, at last, there are people who have no choice, they either get one or the other, sometimes both.

Basically, you are born with a family or a broken family. You absolutely don't have a choice what you are born into in this life.

No one told me that I could choose to be a mixed breed of the human race. I was never told how I could choose what I look like. No one gave me the choice what family and community I was going to be born into. I had no say in what part of the world that I wanted to grow up in.

No one gave me the choice of being bipolar. A wheel that spins that lands you into different sanctions of this game that we all play creates life. But, what you can choose in life is your objective. What is my objective that you may ask? Well, I want to inspire, be free, and most importantly say how I really feel. I can only control my objective. Maybe I have not found the right objective before because I have been so out of touch with life. Breathing the same air as others have helped me see the perspective that I should have been seeing.

Perspective is key. I have never really had a grip on it, but Gray Poopon has set me up to finally understand it a little bit better as an aid to do so. I am here, breathing, moving and living life. Not in some fantasy world that I made up in my head while I was laying on the couch watching some movie.

You cannot choose what you are born into or what has created you, even what has possessed you. No, wait. None of us have a choice at all. You cannot make excuses for any of that. Bipolar disorder cannot be an excuse anymore. It is going to stop, once and for all.

But, you can choose how you want to create your own legacy. It doesn't matter where you come from, because it only matters where you go.

"What the fuck you mad at me for? You don't know anything about me. You don't know what I have been through. I am the King; you are my fool. Shine my shoes, comb my hair, pour my wine and kiss my dime. Look at them jokers, mannequins, and Batman. He's a billionaire earner. Don't make sense. Timmy Turner. Make me a sandwich, spread that Grey Poupon. I wanna feel fresh, not gray and pooped on. I wanna live in a world that we can all get along. I am just taking what God will give me. Having a bad attitude won't let me. Did I lose you? It's okay, I trust you."

3/27/17

Well, I woke up this morning with a minor anxiety attack. This means my body is becoming dependent on my 50 milligrams of Gray Poopon to help me get through this thing called "Life." What I did was that I got out of the house and walked down the street to the coffee shop and grabbed a quick cup of coffee. After walking back and drinking my cup of Joe to my house through the frigid streets of this still very cold weather, I hopped in the shower afterwards and by doing that helped me overcome this minor anxiety attack. A change in environment, walking, and small accomplishments have been a good implemented strategy for me to overcome these sudden anxiety attacks.

After this small triumph this morning, I realized that my celestial sphere is directly overhead. This is my stellar nursery because I am realizing that now I am a star ready to be born. Isn't astronomy beautiful?

3/28/17

Today I realized that I was low on Gray Poopon. I didn't stress at all about it, which is nice because these simple things such as refilling your prescriptions generally stress me out.

I need to come to full closure about Lo Mein. I am over it because I have to be. Without the help of Gray Poopon, I couldn't have ever realized that I was wasting my energy and precious thoughts. If I was not doing my Gray Poopon regiment, mania would have majorly kicked in and my life would be a total mess.

Mania would have caused me to be passionate about her, which I have prevented through my Gray Poopon regiment. So, with the help of a drug called Gray Poopon, I got over a girl that doesn't need my time or attention. The only person that needs my time or attention is myself. I am so proud that I am only focusing my energy on things that I can control.

Honestly, I don't know if those feelings were fabricated by mania or if they were true. The Gray Poopon and the help of my friends, Remy Williams and Nigel Hemingway have really brought me back to earth. What will most likely happen is that I will finally realize that this is not real because she is a muse. Honestly, I am glad that I finally have the clarity to realize these things. But for now, I am using her as inspiration to focus on my creative endeavors.

Every creative person has a muse. The thing with muses is that they fade. Overtime, she will fade away.

I need to get my health to the point where it needs to be so I can be ready for real feelings and emotions on a normal level. When this happens and if I were to reconnect with Lo Mein again, she will be getting the best David Zosel. If she doesn't see that and isn't interested then well, it wasn't meant to be. For now, I want to be friends with that crazy bird. Having her in my life by being friends with her is better than not having her in my life. Right?

Goodbye for now. I have some things to sort out in my life so that you can get the best David Zosel when the time is right or if it permits.

Carrying on, summer is coming. The temperature in Minnesota is hitting the mid 60's this week and my worst nemesis is back in town: the sun.

The sun has been coming up and it gives off this radiant energy that I can thrive off of. This is slowly ensuing mania for me. Last night, I stayed up till three in the morning and I got up at eight for a coffee meeting. Then I had a Government meeting today about a new PTO-Sick Day policy that is being put in place. I had to go to this meeting because it is one of the job responsibilities at the restaurant that I have.

Boy, was I not prepared for how intense this thing was. There were loads and loads of information about this new policy. I was not prepared for it at all, not bringing a notebook, I had to write notes down with my cell phone. I thought this thing was a "coffee and doughnuts", pick up your brochure's kind of deal. No, this was more intensive than any college course that I have ever took.

Unnaturally, I was calm about it and I didn't stress out at all. I don't think I have ever been so focused being in a classroom environment before. It was a life-changing moment for me. Seriously. This is at 50 milligrams. I am sort of excited to see what 100, 150, and 200 milligrams will do. I hope you are interested in seeing that as well.

In conclusion, the sun is out. I got less than four hours of sleep last night and it is five in the afternoon right now. I feel very energized. The thing is, this starts to happen around the end of March every year and then my manic phase starts to wind up and gets into full swing around June. I am very concerned for myself, but hopefully I will be this calm in June and throughout the summer.

But, that is no easy task.

I forget to attribute the importance of Remy Williams, he has inspired me to pick up the guitar and play music again. He and I have played guitar and sang songs together all winter. Performing, learning, singing all help you stay in the moment, which is something that is hard for someone with bipolar disorder. Playing guitar is great because you are moving your left hand, right hand, singing forming a natural chaos in your brain that helps you focus and stay in the moment. Finding something like music really helps center and balance your mental state of mind. If it weren't for him, I wouldn't be playing any music or guitar right now because he is the one that pushes me to learn all of these songs and sing them. Remy Williams is excited about music and learning all about being a singer-songwriter, which excites me as well. I haven't even been remotely as excited as he is but he reminds me of when I first started out learning guitar and singing a few years ago. Personally, I wish that I had a friend at the time to be playing along with me. Going along with Remy Williams has been the best thing for me. This is because we have made our fictitious rock star alter-egos, created a fake band, made ridiculous back-stories about ourselves and even played fake concerts to sell out crowds of 200,000 people. Besides Gray Poopon, the musical arrangement called "Black Dog Run" has been the greatest thing that could have happened to my mental health that has aided me into defeating major depressive episodes during the winter. Thank you, Remy Williams.

Another thing to note, this is what has inspired me to speak in a British accent sometimes, enabling me to relieve my anxiety.

Sounds silly, right? Well, being silly is a great way to relieve your stress, anxiety and depression. Jumping on your bed, dancing with no music, pulling pranks or being a goofball for a little bit each day is a proven way to have temporary relief of what goes on in your head. Whatever that may be.

My British-Australian alter ego, Bosworth "Bozzy" Bentley is the epitome of that. Remy is the "Star" and I am the "Fool" in our band, Black Dog Run. It is the perfect combination, like Ringo Starr and the rest of The Beatles.

My final thoughts for today are about how at this very moment in time, I do not feel dull and gray. I don't feel gray and pooped on at all. I feel as if though I have now survived one of the two phases of bipolar disorder. It is amazing to finally start seeing me thrive a little bit because it can only take off from here. The biggest part is learning how to survive and thrive through mania, which is coming with summer. For once, I can take the massive creative energy that I have and apply it to a controlled focus.

It's as if I am a master of my own domain. Things are looking up and I am ready to roll, baby.

"The sun shines upon the water on the coast and it shines upon the farm fields. Wherever the sun shines it helps the world define. But, summer is coming and so is mania. I don't know how many times that I am going to have to explain to ya that I am a special dude with a special path. I know you know that I am bad at math. But that does not control the life path."

3/30/17

Gray Poopon is not an end all cure all drug. It is merely an aid to helping you become centered. My bipolar tendencies are still here, but you need to have self-control in order to harness its power.

My Mom is a very intense person and it was her week off from work this week. I decided to spend some time with her because if I didn't then I would feel like a terrible son. We went to go shopping for some pants and then we had lunch. The entire time she was talking my ear off about jobs, careers, the restaurant and etc. I could have tuned her out, argued with her, snapped at her and made it a terrible time. Then I realized I had the capability to listen to what she had to say because she doesn't get a chance to talk to me as much as she can, so I'd figure I would listen.

I listened.

It was beautiful.

4/6/17

All I care about is becoming mentally healthy. I can put my dreams of being a filmmaker on hold. There are many dreams that I have, but I guess the only dream that I have when it comes down to it is that I want to be able to turn anything into gold. This is an unrealistic dream. But, the key to achieving any dream for me is to find the right mental health. For one thing, I am light years away from it. Summer hasn't come yet.

There are many phases, interactions, and emotions that I have yet to even scratch. Being rejected, in love, anger, creating new friendships, initiation of relationships are a few things.

Partying, alcohol, work, family issues, hatred, fear, nerves are a few more.

I am very scared that I won't be able to reach my dreams and turn them into reality. But, none of my dreams are achievable with my mental state of mind. The upside to this is that this is the best time in my life to prioritize again all of my dreams. What I will do is take them and make them obtainable. For example, I want to be a filmmaker but I am a better writer. Writing is something that I do all the time. I will continue to write screenplays. Maybe someday I will be behind the camera directing again.

Back in November, I got hired to write a television pilot for a man in Dallas who supposedly has mad connections in the industry. Today, I finished writing it. My goal was to finish this project and I did it. Before the week started, I told myself that I was going to work on a new project each week. So, next week I will work on something new, like painting a goalie mask.

I don't know if anything will come out of this pilot, but I know that I wrote the best 25 pages that I could and for that, I am proud of myself.

My dreams won't be put on hold. I don't think I will ever stop chasing my dreams. But, now since I am more centered and things are put into perspective for me a little bit better, I now realize that everything must be done in moderation.

Baby steps.

Today a pilot, maybe tomorrow a blockbuster. Who knows?

My therapist said I was very brave. No one has ever said that to me before I think. All my life I have been nothing but brave. I guess that is something that people in real life don't get rewarded for like they do in the movies.

My passion is movies and I used to live vicariously through movies. I had to take a lot of time off from watching films to get back into touch with reality. Living life in real time is pretty remarkable.

Life is nothing like the movies. That is for sure.

I have never been called brave before. It really tickled me when she said that because I don't think she has ever said anything about me like that before. It was a beautiful breakthrough for me.

Gray Poopon isn't going to solve all my issues. The only one who can do that for me is myself. Living life in motion is hard and I am finally starting to do it.

Honestly, I thought I was being a coward by not wildly chasing my dreams through using my bipolar disorder as a crutch. Now, I realize that this has been a good thing for me, but never again will I use it as an excuse.Trying to get well since my diagnosis has been my only priority before I can do anything else. I want to be my best self in order to live the best life that I can live.

My bravado brings me bravery. I am brave and I always have been.

Last night, I asked a girl out on a date. I did it sober and on Gray Poopon. It was gratifying because I broke out of a huge shell. I even had major nerves about this too. I never get nervous about these things because my head is usually in the clouds. It was a breakthrough because I was being brave like a normal person.

Whatever a normal person is.

Some mornings when I wake up and I have manageable anxiety attacks. I have never been able to handle them so well before. When this happens, I assure myself by letting myself know that I haven't taken my medication before and that it is working.

These are normal healthy anxiety attacks that normal people have. This only happens when the medicine wears off. When the medicine wears off, I don't panic, I reassure myself that it is working.

For my whole life the issues of mania, delusion, anxiety and depression have haunted me. Again, take two deep breaths really fast, inhaling first then exhaling, then scream. Do this five times fast.

Imagine feeling like that in your brain 90% of your life. Then suddenly that is gone. There aren't 10 trillion ping pong balls rattling in my brain anymore. Instead, at 50 milligrams, these ping pong balls are slowly beginning to drop one at a time, but still in a plethora at sporadic times.

My life was and has been so constantly stressful for me. Every second has been a struggle, because everything stresses me out, causing me to panic all the time. For example, brushing my teeth stresses me out and so does taking a shower. Putting on my shoes stresses me out as well. I hope that those examples convey to you how bad it has always been for me. How can anyone stand the monster that they see in me? I don't even think I could stand being around myself if I was anyone else. So, this Gray Poopon regiment that I am slowly developing is pretty effective. This is because I get to crawl again like a toddler, slowly learning how to walk. Not many people get a second chance like this to crawl. Soon I'll be taking my first steps to success.

I cannot wait for that day.

Eudemonia is a Greek phrase for love and happiness through human flourishing. This provides good for one's self and community through the three types of life: hedonism, honor, and contemplation. As of now, with 50 milligrams of Gray Poopon, I am slowly grasping the mental and physical development of these three types of life.

Bring on the new relationships, careers, opportunities; I am ready.

If you devote your life to achieving the pinnacle of success of good mental health and find a way to maintain that health, then everything else will slowly fall in the right place.

But remember, summer is coming.

I haven't been on Gray Poopon during the summer, a depressive or manic episode, during a crazy stressful time in my life, through a bad break up, a major crisis or anything that could set me back. I know if I can get through summer that this Gray Poopon will be a successful tool for me to succeed.

Right now, I am in a safe zone in my life to take things slow. I am using wisely and I am learning a lot.

The best part of it is, that it isn't overwhelming.

I can do it.

"If I don't dance, I'm making moves."

4/10/17

Butterflies are rumbling in my stomach. Things are going way to smooth. There have been no ups or downs as of late. But, I am nervous because this has never happened to me before in the entirety of my life.

My dosage is about to increase to 100 milligrams of Gray Poopon. That is why I am nervous. It has been eight weeks of a 50 milligrams dosage and it has been working wonders for me thus far. I have been able to keep my creativity flowing, my productivity at a steady rate and for the first time in my life, and continue to be disciplined at a moderate level.

Nerves are really flowing through my veins because summer is coming. Everyone right now is smiling, the beer is flowing, people are wearing shorts and pretending like we live in a fairy tale land of good weather. Well, guess what? It started snowing again. It is April. Minnesota weather is not good for people who struggle with seasonal depression because the seasons here really affect your mental health.

Spring and fall are really tricky seasons because I have always found myself springing back and forth with mania and depression. Last Friday it was super sunny out. I was full of energy and happy as all can be. Today is Monday and it is cold, gray and snowing. Do I really need to tell you what my mood is today?

The thing is, with Gray Poopon, I don't feel so hopeless on this gloomy day. I was able to be productive and have a good start to my week. I did all of my meal prepping, promoted my new article on my blog (TheZosKnows.com), finished my television pilot, prepared for my job interview, and went to the gym and further planned my week.

Thus far, I am proud of myself. My relationships with people are becoming stronger. I have been able to work little by little every day growing the things that I care about. Life is like a garden. It really is because it is a process. My social media following has significantly grown, more people are reading my blog, people are contacting me to write for their publications and this is only the beginning. Right now this is all in its infancy and my blog is beginning to sprout. I am excited to see how much further it can grow.

On the flip side to this coin, all of my workouts are really starting to pay off. By going to the gym every day with Remy Williams, I have grown a lot stronger and I have built a little bit more muscle mass. The both of us have gotten into a regiment of meal prepping for each week so that we have food for breakfast and lunch. This has really shown a huge improvement in our lives because we both have noticed how healthy we feel. Most importantly, working out and eating right has helped my mental health tremendously.

My job search has also gotten a lot better as well. I have an interview coming up within the next week and a half and I am hell bent on getting this new job. Yes, I have major hopes and dreams but I have to be able to support those dreams for now. I had a very important meeting with my Father's friend from high school and he told me that he never got his career started until he was 29 years old. I am 24, but I am not going to compare myself to him. The thing is he told me a very vital thing and that is that he works in order to live rather than living to work. You can be a CEO or you can be a great family man. That is what he is, a family man. The way I look at it is that I don't have a family to support. I want to find a job so I can support my "children", also known as my passions such as filmmaking, blogging, brand creation, entrepreneurial ventures, investments, cooking and traveling. I was always opposed to getting a real "big boy" job before I started taking Gray Poopon. But now I can handle the thought of it and I am open to it. I can't wait to find a new job, meet new people and do new things. Whether I like it or not, I will be making more money with more benefits. So, keep your fingers crossed, I really hope I get this new job.

The biggest news is that I finally finished this television pilot for this guy who hired me to write it. I plan on going once over with it this week and calling the guy, telling him that I'd like to be flown down to Dallas to meet with him. This way, I get to have a little mini vacation in a warm state for a few days. I almost thought I would never finish this pilot. But, being the proficient writer that I am, it only took me one day to finish it. It is pure magic through twenty-four pages. I don't know if anything good will come out of it. Back in December I thought I was going to take over the whole world when I was presented with this opportunity, but now I am proud that I wrote a solid twenty-four pages.

Again, slowly but surely I am proud to say that I am finally starting to begin to incorporate Aristotle's concept of happiness through accomplishment into my life. This is still not mastered and there is a long way to go for me. What I need to do is to find how to not become so thin spread, and even when I do, I need to use moderation in order to slowly accomplish these projects to find happiness through fulfillment.

I am slowly knocking down each domino in my life, one by one. I am thriving slowly but surely. My head is attached to my body and that is the way I like it. But, summer is coming. I don't know what this higher dosage will do for me at all. The coin is up in the air and this is the beginning of my journey towards finding my own well being in life. Summer will be the biggest test because anything we go through is a test of time, trial and error. I do feel confident about summer, but it is a major wild card with my bipolar disorder.

There are so many factors that can effect bipolar disorder and what I am doing right now is trying to master living life with it, trying to master every new situation, emotion and interactions with the new outlook that Gray Poopon has been able to present to me. Honestly, I am going to give Gray Poopon 45% of the credit to the slow success that I am having and the rest of the credit to me, my friends and family. Personally, I have done a lot to change my lifestyle to help my mental health.

You can't take one pill and then "poof" all of your problems are solved. Are you kidding me? Do you think this is "The Matrix" or something?

This is my struggle and I am the master of my domain. I am the only one who can overcome my struggle.

"I'm just a dude that ain't rude. I gotta find a wife so I can live life right. I need a partner that will keep me sharper. Love me till I'm old and prickly. Make me food bought with coupons. A fresh BLT with Grey Poupon. Someone that I can ball with a partner who can let me get my hoop on."

4/11/17

No one cares that you are bipolar. It is not an excuse. Medicated or not, you still are going to be bipolar. People will try to understand you, but most people won't unless they have the same types of things that are going on upstairs as well. Gray Poopon has helped me majorly with my critical "X" factor moments. But, I still have my moments. Yes, those moments where I freak out. When I was younger I was called a "spaz" from third grade till eighth grade, and now I know why.

Honestly, I should go live with Buddhists monks for a year to learn how to be calm and peaceful all the time. Call me a hot head, call me a spaz, call me whatever; I am trying so hard to be cool.

Yes, I have mental health issues that are severe but don't compare them to your own. I am blessed and grateful for all of my life opportunities and for my family. A lot of people who struggle with mental health problems struggle because they can't afford medication, therapy, and do not have a supportive family. I have more than most people do, and my path may be easier than yours but the both of us have one thing in common and that is that we both struggle day to day because our minds play major tricks on us. I would never trade my problems for yours, and it has taken copious amounts of honesty and bravery to write all of this down to share with the world.

Seriously, there are people who are crippled who cannot find work and have to be supported by the government. A person that I went to high school with recently lost his leg in a motorcycle accident, and is getting discharged from the marines. When he was back in town, Remy Williams told me that it was very difficult for him to be in public because of his deformity when they went to grab drinks at a bar. There is no Gray Poopon that can aid him to grow another leg. Remember, you can breathe, you have all four of your limbs and the fact that people like us can struggle to function in society is a beautiful dark twisted notion, and it is glorious.

Embrace the struggle to get better.

Continuing on this idea, author Kurt Vonnegut writes in "Slaughterhouse Five" in one of his most famous illustrations in his novels writes, "Everything was beautiful, and nothing hurt" on a gravestone. Goodness, doesn't that strike a chord with you? We spend all of our lives complaining and dramatizing all of our problems, and when our lives end, we come to peace if we are lucky, realizing how we got that opportunity to live and experience all of the heartbreak, struggle, and pain. The only thing in life that is guaranteed is death. But, it is extremely difficult to stop complaining about your issues or anything in life, but it is good to know that all of the pain is quite a dubiously beautiful thing because one day it will all go away and it won't hurt anymore.

Moving on, ABC. Always be cool. Bruce Lee is one of my biggest idols because he was so disciplined and cool. He was always calm, cool and collective. Looking back at my entire life, my relationships would have been stronger and I would have had better experiences if I had been more even-keeled.

I don't think I have ever gone a day or two during the entirety of my life where I didn't have a mood swing that caused me to panic and freak out. I guess that is the way I am wired due to my bipolar disorder. But, I can improve on this and get better. It might take me years to master and if my Father can do it; I sure as hell can.

Why am I lamenting again? Well, summer is coming, and it worries me. My dosage is about to increase and am realizing that this Gray Poopon is not going to make me more "Zen" like than I thought I would. Maybe it will, who knows? But, I know it can set me up to be more "Zen" like. The ball is in my court when it comes down to it. Gray Poopon is only there to aid me to help save myself from the way I tend to be.

I mean, if I am always having random freak outs or whatever, who in the hell is going to want to be around me? Who would want to date or marry me? Who would want to be friends with me? I don't even want to be around myself if I were to watch myself from a different vantage point. Being bipolar isn't an excuse.

I'm tired of that being an excuse. This needs to stop. Employers don't care; your girlfriend, friends, strangers and family don't care. There are no excuses in life. Remy Williams always calls me out for giving stupid excuses about stupid things that I do. That needs to stop for me.

No more excuses because I need to learn how to nod my head and accept my mistakes in life. It is hard for me to swallow my pride, but now I gradually own up to my mistakes, enabling me to become a better person in this nebulous state of life that I am in. Due to what I am trying to accomplish, someday I will be reborn again out of the stellar nursery that is guiding me to be a star in this world. Within this nebula, I am slowly traveling to that nursery because of the eudemonia that is developing in my life. I am ten percent there, which is a lot farther than I have been when I started taking Gray Poopon.

I was born to win, and that is what I will do gently.

My life may seem like it is two steps forward, one step back. But remember, I am still going one step forward.

Contact and Inquires

This is my first part of Zosel's documented journey and he has discovered many other things on how to combat mental illnesses with and without medication throughout the next two volumes that he will be releasing.

If you would like to speak with him over the phone or video chat, he is providing very important advice to help you with your situation. If you suffer from a mental illness, or need help understanding someone that you care about with a mental illness, he can help.

Although he is not a therapist, he can provide crucial advice and strategy in order to find balance in your life.

First and foremost, he is here to listen to what you are going through.

Prices:
60 minute session: $50
30 Minute session: $35
Three-session package: $135

Last, Zosel is willing to speak to and for any groups, podcasts, television and radio appearances, give presentations, and to speak during any public speaking engagements.

*All prices for services are negotiable.

For all inquires about these services, please contact me at:
D.Zosel27@Gmail.Com

If you enjoyed "Gray Poopon" be sure to check out his website for weekly blog posts that he writes: TheZosKnows.com

Volume 2: Summertime Mania

"Gray Poopon", the first volume of "Conquering the Gifted Curse of Bipolarism" was written in the winter, a severe time of depression for Zosel. Volume Two will document Zosel's time battling mania. He will be going from 50 to 100 milligrams in his quest. In "Gray Poopon", I figured out how to fight his depressive cycle. Mania is way too fun, but dangerous. Stay tuned to follow Zosel's journey of balance in his life with the aid of Gray Poopon.

Here is a small excerpt from the next volume:

5/7/17

Gray Poopon is helping me with my crazy mood swings because it's keeping me underneath the lines of the bipolar spectrum. If I were to go into an 8x8x8 room and throw a ball, it would go back and forth between the two walls. That is exactly happening with my mood; swaying back and forth between dysthymia and hypomania, sometimes even stopping in the middle grounds. The Gray Poopon is allowing me to stay grounded and preventing me from hitting severe depression or even worse, a manic episode. We don't want mania.

I've lost a lot of friends through mania. That is because not too many people know how to deal with it at all. It is a monster that can scare people away. This is because of the "EEE", my excitement, energy, and enthusiasm is so much more abundantly higher than most people that it frightens everyone to the point where they want to keep a ten foot distance from me.

I now understand that no one will be as excited as me. Most people tread cautiously outside of their comfort zone, where as I have always jumped in the pool immediately. This is because I have always been outside of my comfort zone during my life, and that gave me the attitude of being so uncomfortable that I didn't care anymore. That is why I have this thrill seeking mentality that does not stay within itself. But now, with the aid of Gray Poopon, I am finally discovering what my comfort zone is and what it means to me. But yet, it is very foreign because I have finally scratched the surface of it.

About the Author

Residing in Minneapolis, Minnesota, David Zosel is a writer, filmmaker, brand strategist, and a family restaurant owner of Kings Wine Bar. Suffering from severe Bipolar I disorder, he

writes every day to find balance and peace. This is his first published book, and he plans on publishing many more works about mental health in order to help others, understand your loved ones with mental health issues, and to provide valuable information to students, psychiatrists, and therapists all over the world. Zosel also plans on pursuing a career as a writer who writes in a variety of mediums in literature. Zosel enjoys playing hockey, watching films, and eating pizza and Asian cuisine. He blogs about a variety of topics such as mental health, The Minnesota Vikings, and self-discoveries about the world on his website, TheZosKnows.com.

Photo Credit: Shane Hudak
Sphotostudio.com

78258928R00077

Made in the USA
Lexington, KY
06 January 2018